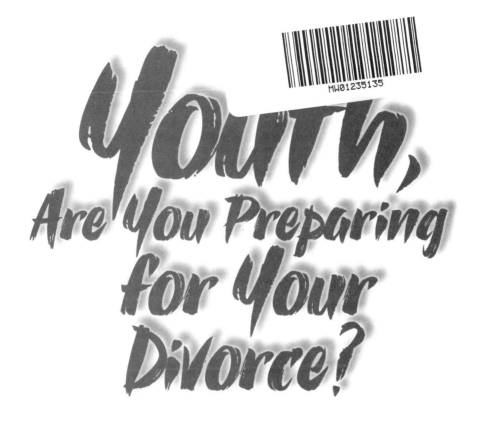

Youth, Are You Preparing for Your Divorce?

BY

Colin D. Standish
President of Hartland Institute

AND

Russell R. Standish
Administrator of Highwood College and Health Centre

Cover design / illustration by

Ron J. Pride, square1studio

ISBN 0-923309-96-9

A Division of Hartland Institute

Box 1, Rapidan, VA 22733, U.S.A.

www.hartlandpublications.com

Contents

1
Old Men; Wise Counsel

SOME teenagers and even their parents may wonder how two seventy-two-year-olds would have relevant counsel to offer to teenagers. After all, we grew up in an age when society was greatly different from the society of today. However, we have seen the transition from a society when even those with little Christian interest held to very firm moral principles, when divorce and separation were uncommon. Yet the morals of society today are greatly different. Even among practicing Christians, some have scant regard for biblical morality. Many "Christians" live together out of wedlock, divorce is epidemic, and homosexual and lesbian "marriages" are considered acceptable by significant numbers of Christians who believe in permissive abortion and premarital sex, and even that adulterous relations can be accommodated within the community of Christian believers.

Because we have lived in these vastly contrasting societies we bring to this book the experience we have gained through the passage of time. We know at first hand the consequences of accepting entirely different value systems. Without a doubt, the affluent, free moral spirit of today has harvested a generation which is much more subject to insecurity, instability, depression, unhappiness and dysfunctional behaviors.

In the western world, for the most part, there was a strong adherence to the moral principles of the absolutes of the Ten Commandments during the nineteenth century. However, many soon thereafter were rejecting, or at least ignoring, God's commandments, and so society became governed by the changing moral values of social mores. At first these mores were little different from God's principles and moral values. Thus when we were children and youth, though many of our neighbors showed little or no interest in church or its activities, yet they fiercely guarded the moral reputation of their families. Daughters were firmly warned not to disgrace the family by any form of premarital sexual activity and male teens were admonished to respect young ladies and to protect the moral integrity of their female escorts. Most young men expected their wives to be virgins at the marriage altar.

However, without the absolutes of God's commandments, soon the social mores began to slip. Rapidly what we call in this book the "Hollywood Syndrome" took over. As movies, television programs, internet images and magazines boldly ravaged the barriers of decent society, moral values plummeted and any thoughts of God's principles, even in many churches, evaporated.

We have bridged these two eras. With the experience of many years, we have gained much from the perspective of hindsight. We have not only been witnesses to the tearing down of societal moral fabric, but we have seen the shocking consequences of these changes in modern society.

Often using the euphemism of liberation from the "prudish" Victorian era, many of this generation have embraced the so-called "sexual revolution" in which scant respect is paid to those who dare to condemn all forms of sexual immorality including premarital sex, extramarital sex, homosexuality, lesbianism, and bestiality. Only rape, incest and pedophile sex seem still off limits for now. Even as we write there are those urging the lowering of the age for consensual sex in the United Sates to 14. How blind are these advocates of the practice of juvenile sex! How ignorant are they of the lifelong negative emotional, social and family consequences which are the result of such practices. Or do they even care!

Russell as a physician well remembers the sexual revolution of the 1960s. Unsanctified persons, disdaining the loving and wise counsels of God as set forth in the seventh commandment of the Law of God, claimed that we had entered the era of sexual liberation. God's Word in the seventh commandment states plainly: "Thou shalt not commit adultery." (Exodus 20:14)

That commandment prohibited all forms of sex outside a consenting, loving marriage relationship. Christ, Himself, illustrated the broad nature of the seventh commandment.

> But I say unto you, That whosoever looketh on a woman to lust after her hath committed adultery with her already in his heart.   Matthew 5:28

Perhaps no one person has been more responsible for the sexual revolution in society than Dr. Alfred Kinsey, who published his two reports on human sexuality in 1948 and 1953. These studies hit at the very heart of Biblical morality and opened the flood gate to immorality which has yielded a harvest of grief and tragedy to the human race. It has resulted in emotional breakdowns, divorces, suicides, abortions and perversions on a massive scale.

The sexual liberation mind-set was greatly facilitated by two scientific discoveries. In 1929, Sir Alexander Fleming, a bacteriologist, discovered penicillin while working at St. Mary's Hospital in London, a world famous old medical institution. Russell well remembers this hospital, for it was there that he undertook the critical oral section of examination, under exacting examiners, when sitting for his specialty degree, the membership of the Royal College of Physicians of the United Kingdom. It was also here that Princes William and Harry were born to Princess Diana, the former wife of Prince Charles, Prince of Wales.

Penicillin led to loss of the fear of venereal disease which had provided a strong barrier against immorality. Russell treated hundreds of cases of gonorrhea in that period. A simple injection of penicillin cured every case. Syphilis required 14 injections of Penicillin for certain cure. Thus the fear of death, insanity, blindness and many other fearful consequences of venereal diseases disappeared.

The second scientific discovery, a little later, was that of the contraceptive pill. This took away the fear of pregnancy in women. Thus it was claimed that promiscuous sexual relations could be entered into without any lasting consequences.

None should doubt the love and wisdom of God, for He foresaw the fearful epidemic of herpes genitalis which increases the incidence of cancer of the womb fivefold. There is still no cure. He knew that another presently incurable disease, AIDS, would destroy millions of persons. Surely no one can question the word of Scripture which twice declared in a single chapter, that "God is love" (1 John 4:8, 16).

It has been most distressing for Russell to treat victims of both these diseases. The term "sexual liberation" soon faded into the dustbin of archaic English expressions.

Today's society panders to the "do what comes naturally" concept. Everything is done to provide youth with the "freedom" to experience any form of sex, including vile practices of perversion, without fearing the consequences. Freely available are the pill before and the pill the day after, the condom, and the abortion clinic. However, the reckoning of the spiritual, social, emotional and physical consequences are all but ignored except by the most perceptive researchers and those who well understand the shattering spiritual consequences of the principle of free love.

In some countries of the western world it is a crime to promote Biblical morality by declaring publicly the perversity of homosexuality for example. Governments are legalizing same sex partnerships. Employers are forced to offer family benefits to those who choose to live a gay lifestyle. Hate laws and anti-vilification laws have been enforced in various countries, and those violating these laws are punished with penalties of harsh fines, and in some cases, imprisonment.

Such laws violate the conscience of dedicated, sincere, Bible-believing Christians who see it as their God-given responsibility to warn young people of the eternal consequences of living a life of promiscuity. These laws fly in the face of the clearest testimony of Holy Scripture, which admonishes all with these words:

> Flee also youthful lusts: but follow righteousness, faith, charity, peace, with them that call on the Lord out of a pure heart.   2 Timothy 2:22

Paul understood that these lusts are especially tempting to the wealthy class. Those who live in the west are particularly vulnerable. Therefore the following text has deep significance to the youth of the affluent west.

> But they that will be rich fall into temptation and a snare, and into many foolish and hurtful lusts, which drown men in destruction and perdition.
>   1 Timothy 6:9

So permissive is contemporary society that many professing Christian youth are confused about moral parameters. All too frequently they have scant help from their parents, from their church and Christian schools. They receive little clear guidance from persons who would rather comfort those who have fallen into shameful behaviors than to courageously explain to youth the true principles of Biblical morality. Many a youth, who otherwise would have formed a foundation for a lifetime of faithful service for God and man, has so tarnished his or her reputation and thereby has been filled with guilt and despair, that he or she never fulfills the potential for godly service. Some are so devastated and ashamed that they never again walk with the Lord.

We have a great love for children and youth. Russell is the father of three sons now in their early and mid-forties. Colin has a son 23 and a daughter 20 years of age. We both are trained educators; we both are trained psychologists. Russell is a trained physician. Colin and Russell have taught in primary (elementary) schools in Australia. Both have taught at the University of Sydney. Colin has been the chairman of a college education department in Australia and the president of a Christian college in Jamaica, and has headed three Christian colleges in the United States. Colin has completed his fifty-fourth year in Education. Russell has been a president of two Christian hospitals, in Thailand and Malaysia, and has served at other hospitals. Both are presently leading Christian training Colleges; Russell in Australia and Colin in the United Sates.

We both have a great interest in young people. We have a special desire to see that young people know the true principles of Christian living, and also the all-important way to live successfully by these principles, which are the keys to successful marriages and therefore the pathway to fulfillment and happiness.

We believe this book will be a source of great certainty to all who read it, both young and the parents of the youth. It will answer many questions you have in your minds and possibly questions that you may yet not have asked, because every principle of this book is built upon the counsel of the Bible and supported by the findings of scientific studies. God bless you all as you prayerfully read this book.

2

How to Avoid Divorce

THE cynic declares, "The easiest way to avoid a divorce is never to be married." However, we doubt that this likely will be the route that you will choose. Some do, however, make the decision to live together without the sanctity of the marriage commitment. As we will see later in this book, that is not the God-given solution, neither is it likely to provide secure happiness nor the permanency of a secure family life.

Marriage is a sacred ordinance established by God Himself. Indeed we go back to the beginning of the human race as recorded in Genesis, chapter 2, where there are only two enduring institutions which came from the Garden of Eden. The first was the institution of the weekly Sabbath.

> Thus the heavens and the earth were finished, and all the host of them. And on the seventh day God ended his work which he had made; and he rested on the seventh day from all his work which he had made. And God blessed the seventh day, and sanctified it: because that in it he had rested from all his work which God created and made.   Genesis 2:1–3

The second is the ordinance of marriage.

> And the Lord God caused a deep sleep to fall upon Adam, and he slept: and he took one of his ribs, and closed up the flesh instead thereof; And the rib, which the Lord God had taken from man, made he a woman, and brought her unto the man. And Adam said, This is now bone of my bones, and flesh of my flesh: she shall be called Woman, because she was taken out of Man. Therefore shall a man leave his father and his mother, and shall cleave unto his wife: and they shall be one flesh.   Genesis 2:21–24

There are many promises, commitments, covenants and vows which we are likely to make throughout life. Clearly, the most sacred vow any human being can take is the vow to love, honor, serve and obey God throughout this life and the eternal life to come.

The second most sacred vow which we take is the marriage vow. It is a vow taken before God and in the presence of witnesses, be they few or many, a vow which the authors took at their marriage and, as gospel ministers, vows which we have placed before many young people standing before the altar of God, pledging lifelong allegiance to each other. We have spent much time before the marriage service with those who are planning to marry. We present all the finest Christian principles we know in the hope that we will secure the success of the marriage. We are happy to say that most of the marriages which we have performed continue to be strong and successful. Sadly, however, there have been exceptions in spite of our best efforts. In these cases our premarital counseling has not been sufficient to secure the permanency of the marriage.

We recognize that there are many innovative and sometimes frivolous vows which are taken at the marriage altar today. We, however, believe strongly in the vows long used, which we place in great solemnity before those planning to be married. The vow to "Take this woman (or this man) to be your lawfully wedded wife (or husband), to love, honor and cherish her (him) until death do you part, in prosperity or in adversity, in sickness or in health and to keep her (him) only unto yourself as long as you both shall live," has stood the test of time.

So often in the euphoria of marriage preparation and the excitement of the marriage itself, the vow is taken very lightly. The implications of that vow may not be seriously considered. When a young, handsome and virile man is standing at the altar, the young lady may find it very difficult to contemplate that sometime in the future he might be a cripple in a wheel-chair or that he may lose his mind. The young man standing beside the young lady of his dreams in all her youthful beauty, may not seriously con-template what it means when the bloom of youth fades and the aging pro-cess takes its toll on her beauty and her physical form. This is why, while physical and intellectual attractiveness have significant appeal, they can-not be the major component in the choice of a spouse. There must be those deeper, enduring values which can come only when, while understanding all the things which can happen, we nevertheless have the deepest of love for our spouse. This is why Christian principles provide the perfect bases for a loving and fruitful marriage. This is why this book is directed to sav-ing young people from taking those steps in courtship which will prepare them for divorce in the future.

3

Emotional Turmoil

BETTY was in deep emotional turmoil when she entered Colin's office. She was a student at the Christian college of which he was then president. He knew her husband, Bob, also a student at the college, less well, though at least he had passed pleasantries with him on two or three occasions. The couple had been married less than one year when Betty came in tears to Colin's office, obviously greatly distressed. She politely asked if Colin had time to give her a little counsel. Soon she revealed the cause of her distress. She had just discovered that Bob was deep into an affair with another young woman. Her agony of heart was greatly intensified by the fact that she was already pregnant with their child. She was wholly shocked that her much beloved husband had so soon after their marriage found his attentions turned to another woman. This infidelity threatened to result in yet another tragic marital catastrophe.

Betty and Bob could be listed as a statistic amongst the millions of divorces around the world every year. As with so many others, Betty's dreams had evaporated in one brief segment of time. Her future had crashed to the ground. Thoughts flooded through her mind. Would there be any way to save the marriage? What could she do with the little one, yet to be born? To what kind of a life could she look forward if Bob left permanently? Should she go back to live with her parents? What should she do about her college education and her aspirations to serve God as a nurse? Was there anyone who could help her? In whom should she confide? How should she approach Bob? These and many other questions were whirling in her troubled mind. Betty had had not the slightest intimation that Bob was not faithful to the marriage until his extramarital affair was revealed to her by a close friend. In that one moment of time her world crumbled and fell apart.

Colin was well aware that it is improper for a minister to counsel one of the opposite sex upon such issues. As soon as he learned the nature of the visit of this dear woman to his office, he arranged with the Dean of Women, a godly Christian, to assist her in her plight. Whether the marriage ever came back together again, Colin does not know, for not long after this incident he transferred to lead another college. One thing was evident: she still loved her husband dearly.

As Colin lent a very sympathetic ear to Betty while she unfolded her plight, her story unraveled. Both Betty and Bill had been terribly hurt emotionally in their teenage years when their parents divorced. In both cases they had felt the anguish of parents, both of whom they loved, parents with whom they desired to live as a family. Both their parents had slipped into separation and ultimately divorce. In each case, while one parent earnestly desired the continuation of the marriage, the other was determined, in middle life, to seek a new spouse and begin a new life.

The tragedy was heightened by the fact that in both cases the parents had managed to keep the fragility of their marriages from their children until just prior to the separations. Both Betty and Bob had witnessed scenes that were tense and had heard angry words on occasions but they had no thought that a separation or divorce was imminent. They had both been torn by their dual loyalties. They had both felt that each parent was seeking to win their loyalty away from the other spouse. They were subject to the explanations that each parent gave to assure them that the other parent was at fault. This only added to their pain, which resulted in a significant drop in their academic performance in school. At the time, before they had reached the middle of their teenage years, they vainly sought to distance themselves from the pressure of each parent seeking to gain the loyalty of their children by discrediting the other parent. Having both gone through such an experience in homes claiming to be Christian based, these young people had determined in their minds that they would never allow the same thing to happen to them.

When they met at college they were quickly attracted to each other, before knowing the common plight of the other as teenagers. As they found time to know each other better, however, they realized that both of them had faced quite similar experiences with the devastating split in their families. Of course, each could understand the pain that the other had experienced and each was drawn to the other, understandably, by a common bond that often develops when two young people have encountered similar emotional trauma.

These were intelligent young people. They knew that statistics showed that children who came from broken homes were themselves more likely to have marriages which ended in divorce proceedings. They also knew that when both partners of a marriage come from troubled homes, the risks are even greater. So as earnest Christians they decided that they would be very careful in preparation for marriage, for they both believed that they were being drawn to the marriage altar. They spent many hours together, studying the counsels of the Scripture and reading the advice and counsel from authors who had addressed the issue of marriage preparation. They had prayed earnestly that God would keep them faithful to each other. Each had many times, long before taking the formal marriage vows, earnestly assured the other that nothing would break their loyalty in marriage.

As Betty spoke, Colin's heart ached for her, a truly lovely young lady who loved her Savior. However, in her bewilderment, she could not understand how the infidelity of her husband could have possibly happened. She believed in spite of the trouble of their youth, that they had so carefully prepared for the marriage, and made such firm and sincere commitments to each other, that nothing would split them apart. But that had not been the case. Maybe their decision had been too dependent upon this one common thread. Almost certainly Betty's commitment to Christ had been much more complete than that of Bob, as his infidelity testified.

We talked of the possibility of Bob coming to talk with Colin where they could counsel together. She dearly desired this. However, later, she told Colin that Bob did not desire such counseling. That was a very poor sign. Another marriage was on the way to shipwreck. The reality is that once a spouse has made up his or her mind to separate from the other spouse it is extraordinarily rare that the best counselors or the wisest advisors can alter this intention. Generally, by the time the counseling stage is reached, the one desiring to sever the marriage commitment is not likely to change. This does not mean that any effort should be spared, for there are exceptions, as both of us have seen. This book is designed to set forth the steps which can be taken in preparation, during the early years of life, which will reduce greatly the likelihood of a marriage which will later splinter. What are the subtle signs and indications that a marriage has problems which, if not addressed early, may drift to ultimate separation and divorce? We earnestly pray that this book will be a significant help to young people to avoid the likelihood of divorce in their future lives.

However, we must go further. We do not desire that you enter into marriages that endure in the midst of unhappiness. We desire to help you forge a marriage of great fulfillment, where the bonds of happiness are cemented in true love and fidelity based upon true Christian principles.

4

I Can't Live Without You

BRIAN saw himself as something of a Casanova. He acted as if he could not imagine that any young lady could resist his masculine charm. He possessed an outgoing personality. He was professionally trained at a major university. He had a good position and in a short time became nationally known in his field which gave him the opportunity to travel far and wide. He evidenced the fact that he fully believed that what Brian wanted, Brian could get, whether it was in his profession, in his political ambitions or in his romantic pursuits. Eventually he set his eyes on Margaret.

She was a little older than Brian and, for him, that added to her allure. But to Brian's dismay, Margaret failed to show the same amorous leanings to him as he did to her. Perhaps a lesser pursuer would have given up. But not Brian. The more coolly Margaret received his romantic advances, the more persistent he became. He was not used to such rebuffs. There is little doubt that his ego was very much dented by Margaret's disinterest in his attention to her. The more she rejected his advances, the more determined he was to triumph in his quest.

Eventually his relentless pursuit paid dividends and Margaret surrendered to his persistent, determined advances. They were subsequently married. In the early years of the marriage it seemed that, in spite of what had commenced as a one-sided romance, the marriage had actually blossomed into a successful union. Three girls were born to the couple and it was obvious to their friends that Margaret became a very adoring and loving wife. However, as the children were reaching towards their early teen years, rumors surfaced concerning the fidelity of Brian. Brian hotly denied any disloyalty to his wife, claiming that by nature he was friendly, claiming that there was nothing more than platonic friendship with any of the women who were now being associated with him. In spite of his protests the rumors persisted.

There is only so long that a womanizer can continue to deny his activities. It becomes increasingly obvious to wife and family that at unusual hours father was not at home. It is only a short time that a man can hide behind the excuse of his busy work load, or the special projects that he has to accomplish, as the reason for his late home arrivals. And so it was with Brian. Soon his protesting ceased as his wife realized he was pursuing a very vigorous affair with another woman. Heartbroken, she sought every way she knew to help heal the breach. She urged him to seek a counselor or at least to talk it over. But all her pleadings fell upon deaf ears.

When the issue was raised, Brian's response was ever more angry, and that anger turned to violent outbursts which became increasingly part of the environment of his family. He became angry with his wife, accusing her over the most trivial issues following the predictable pattern in such circumstances where the offending spouse seeks to find all manner of flaws in his wife in his efforts to justify his infidelity. Citing the frequent disagreements that now were a part of the marriage, Brian declared that he was leaving. He could not take the misery of living with his family. Of course, never was there any admission that he was the major contributor to that misery. Any misery that he was experiencing was minor compared with the anguish of heart of his spurned spouse.

Brian eventually set a day for the movers to come to take out his possessions from the home. Colin received a desperate phone call from Margaret. She could not bear to lose this man who was unworthy of her. She pled for Colin to come to lunch the day he had set for the moving and that he did. It was one of the most painful experiences of Colin's life. With the three children, Margaret and Brian, Colin sat down to lunch. As the meal was concluding the movers came. With anguished cries Margaret pled with Brian not to leave, but to stay. The children made pleas. But all to no avail.

When the movers came they loaded his furniture. After the movers had left, Colin took Brian for a drive a little way from the home. Brian, however, had set his course in concrete. Nothing which Colin said could now influence him.

Brian represents a breed of men and sometimes women who will pursue a romance with more than normal vigor. This especially becomes apparent when more than love is involved, but when self and ego are additional motivations. Some go beyond Brian's amorous pursuit of Margaret with pleadings "I can't live without you." Such selfish appeals should be immediately and decisively rejected. The selfish motives which lead to the "I can't live without you" proclamation are exactly the same motives which, after marriage, will lead to the protest that, "I can't live with you."

Some go so far as to say, "If you won't marry me, I'll destroy myself." These cruel forms of quest should be absolute proof that the pursuer is unfit for marriage. These are not the words of a true lover. The man who loves a woman or a woman who loves a man will be free from selfish goals, ego striving or pride of victory. Rather, the true lover will love the other to the extent that selflessly he or she would step aside if it were clear that the one who is the object of his or her affection does not show the same response in reciprocation.

Though certainly it is a difficult situation, nevertheless, Christians will understand that someone else may come into his/her life whose selfless love will be reciprocated and who will respond in such a way that there will be evidence of happiness in a future marriage which will last through the ups and downs of life. Those who are fully surrendered to the will of God in this most important decision will rest content that God will lead them to the one who will best complement them in their future marriage. No one should surrender to the pressured plans of an unstable suitor. Sympathy is not a reason for accepting a marriage proposal. The young lady who is wise will not seek to help a needy young man, for all too frequently such young men soon are dependent, then obsessed, resulting in the greatest of emotional dependency. These young men should be helped by young men or older adults where the risks are less. The same principle manifestly applies when a young man is sought by a young woman possessing similar personality defects.

5

What Are the Marriage Stakes?

THE wedding day is naturally a much anticipated occasion. Even for the most godly young woman there is much preparation, many decisions to make, and careful planning which involves a significant number of people. Scripture sets forth marriage days as important events. Almost inevitably, the mother of the bride becomes deeply involved in the preparations. So too do siblings and the extended family members. Some of them will probably be chosen to participate in the wedding service.

It is wise to choose a godly minister to perform the wedding; one who counsels the couple extensively before marriage and faithfully ministers to them after they are married. In the wedding service he will also labor to make an impact upon those who are present, both Christian and nonChristian.

1. There are many issues at stake. When a man and woman have united their lives in holy matrimony, first and foremost at stake is the fulfillment of the lives of the contracting parties. A marriage can bring lifelong love, support and rewarding companionship. The wife should be the best friend of the husband and he the best friend of the wife, where neither dominates nor controls the other and yet where the appropriate Biblical roles of a husband and a wife, a father and a mother are truly fulfilled. Russell often speaks to husbands of "their girlfriend." Some husbands protest. "Hey! She's my wife." Russell's response to this indignation is, "It is a very serious matter if your wife has ceased to be your girlfriend."

2. Ultimately eternal destinies are at stake. First and foremost, the husband has a constant responsibility to do everything to help his wife to be ready for the kingdom of God. But just as surely, the wife shares that responsibility for her husband's salvation. Marriage on earth should be a prelude to the marriage of the Lamb, Christ Jesus. Marriage can have complete success only if the husband and the wife are preparing their lives for the eternal kingdom. More is at stake than the eternal life of the consenting marriage partners. The partnership must have an impact for the salvation of the children who will be entrusted to the family. Nothing will be more beautiful in heaven than to see the parents and children united in the eternal kingdom under the blessed leadership of Jesus. This goal must ever be uppermost in the minds of those who agree to join together in sacred marriage. However, the influence extends far beyond this. It extends to other relatives and the influence and earnest prayers of the couple for the witness they need to convey to the extended families of the husband and the wife. It further encompasses the community, for a husband and wife should form an effective witnessing team to the world. It goes even beyond this to the strangers with whom they come in contact. Every home which is established should be a lighthouse for truth and righteousness, where the Holy Spirit is ministering and where there are angels, not only to protect, but also to guide the footsteps of the marriage partners. God is in command! Tremendous issues are at stake!

3. The greatest tragedies have occurred because of the fractionation of homes. Few people, even claimed Christians, take seriously the responsibility of marriage. Too many couples marry to legitimize uncontrolled passions, sexual indulgence and even perversion. It is irresponsible for such unconverted motives to lead into marriage. The marriage is perverted when physical issues of marriage dominate over the spiritual. Sensual motives arise out of selfishness and lead to uncontrolled indulgence, and frequently result in unconcern for the other partner. When these areas of indulgence are not fully met, discontent arises and this makes it easy to allow the thoughts to deviate from the vows of loyalty which were taken so solemnly at the marriage altar. This is a frequent result when one spouse drifts into unhappiness within the marriage and believes that he/she has a right to be dissatisfied with the other spouse.

From this perilous point it is a short step either to become vulnerable to the advances of a third person or, alternatively, to make advances to a third person. All this can be justified to the carnal mind but it can never be entertained in the mind of a converted man nor woman. So often, in such circumstances, not only is the marriage relationship of the couple in great jeopardy, but also that of another couple, the spouse of whom has either attracted the attention of one of the first couple or, alternatively, has been the object of ungodly attention.

4. The emotional health of the individuals is at stake. A marriage built on principles other than the divine mandates, is a marriage which is very vulnerable—vulnerable to all the attacks of Satan, vulnerable to all the inroads of worldly thinking, passion and unrestrained emotions. Instead of bringing peace and love, contentment, joy and fulfillment, the emotions of discouragement, discontent, unfulfilled hopes and eventually jealousy, envy and even hatred are generated in the heart of one who should possess only tender love for his/her spouse.

5. The influence of a marriage is not confined only to the husband and wife, their happiness and their eternal destiny, nor even to the happiness and eternal destiny of the children. It has a profound influence on the generations yet unborn. It is wise to ask the question, Why is there so little true Christianity in the world today, especially in the western nations? This was not the case in generations past. Let us look at the nations of Western Europe. Most citizens of these nations never, or very rarely, attend church, never pray, never read the Bible, and have given themselves over to the carnal pursuits of the world. Here is the key to the ever-escalating divorce statistics in our society.

It was not so in generations past. Christianity was alive in the sixteenth century, fired by the fervor of the Protestant Reformation—a fervor which affected the majority of homes and impacted upon each one. It was at this time that the Bible became available to the common people as the result of the printing press invented by Gutenberg. Also it was the determination of the Reformers that all children be provided with an education so that they could read and study the Word of God for themselves. It was considered a wonderful privilege, and their gatherings for worship were often over-crowded. We cannot forget preaching in Bethlehem Chapel where John Huss, the great Bohemian (Czech) Reformer thundered the Truths of God. Huss attracted three thousand people weekly, all of whom stood shoulder to shoulder, to hear his powerful three-hour-long discourses calling the people to holiness of life and to following the Scriptures. Nor can we forget preaching in the Lutterworth church, England, where people worshipped in great numbers in order to hear the mighty preaching of John Wycliffe at the end of the fourteenth century and to learn the depths of their Savior's love. What has happened to the children, grandchildren, great-grandchildren and following generations in Europe, so that now there is so little concern for the things of God? Surely generations of parents became less and less committed to God and thus failed to pass on to succeeding generations the values of genuine Christianity.

6. Another circumstance has entered into society—the rapid increase in affluence since the beginning of the industrial revolution through to the technological revolution of the present days. History attests that few can retain their dedication to God when they are living in affluence and worldly comforts. Jesus said,

> It is easier for a camel to go through the eye of a needle, than for a rich man to enter into the kingdom of God.   Matthew 19:24

Also, "Christians" have become engrossed in all forms of entertainment; and with the increased discretionary funds which most Western people have today, it is easy to squander that income for selfish gratification and transitory excitement. The realities of the eternal home are forgotten. The infinite sacrifice of Christ is ignored. The peace and contentment which results from fellowship with the Lord is lost. Therefore godly young men and women have to reestablish homes which are patterned upon the divine paradigm. Too much is at stake to permit our children to grow up controlled by the pitifully low standards of modern-day society. The stability of society and the nation is at stake. The nation is made up of individuals. These individuals help forge families. Families form communities, communities form larger societies which then impact upon the moral fiber and stability of the nation. The greatest reformation called for today is a reformation in the home. The home can be helped by Christian schools and by churches. However, ultimately, many Christian schools and churches, affected by the compromise of individuals and families, simply reflect the depravity of the homes. These agencies of God find it difficult to achieve higher standards than those of the individuals comprising them.

7. There is a final consequence. We delay the return of Jesus. The Word of God calls us to hasten the coming of Jesus.

> Looking for and hasting unto the coming of the day of God.   2 Peter 3:12

This text implies that we can delay the return of Jesus. Our marriage can either hasten the coming of Christ, or it may delay His coming. The home is established so that we will seek to live and witness to the power of Christ. Then such a home will hasten the coming of Jesus.

If a poor choice of the marriage partner is made, the consequences can be devastating, not only to the immediate lives of the individuals, but also to Jesus Christ's return. The solution to this world is the return of Jesus and the establishment of the kingdom of righteousness. Poor marriages hinder that return. Without Christ's return there is no permanent solution in this world. The world desperately needs families totally surrendered to Him and to His will. The family which will be united in truth and righteousness, families who would rather die than dishonor their Lord by committing one wrong word or action, families who have overcome "by the blood of the Lamb, and by the word of their testimony" (Revelation 12:11), will hasten the coming of Jesus.

6

The Invincible Marriage

RARELY will you hear the adjective "invincible" preceding the word "marriage." Many marriages have proven fragile, if not disastrous. It would take a very bold person to assure a young couple that the marriage which they are undertaking is invincible. By invincible we mean that there is no possibility that the marriage will be violated by infidelity or any indiscretions—a marriage where the integrity of both spouses will remain inviolate—a marriage where divorce is never contemplated and separation is never considered—a marriage where the love of the spouses for God and each other increases constantly throughout the duration of the marriage—a couple where both live unwaveringly their marriage vows to "love, honor, cherish till death do us part and keep thee only [exclusively] unto myself as long as we both shall live. In sickness and in health, in prosperity and in adversity." How can it be possible, before the marriage takes place, to declare that this marriage will fulfill these criteria of invincibility?

When we were lads it was not uncommon to hear statements such as "They are the perfect couple." Today, only someone very audacious would make such an unreserved statement, and therefore such statements are rarely heard and, if made, are often adjudged to be hyperbole, if not gross recklessness and outrageous exaggeration. However, we believe that true Christian marriages can be invincible no matter what adversities or tragedies may come into the marriage. There are those who would say that only perfect people could have an invincible marriage. This phrase gets very close to the issue!

Unfortunately, today the vast majority of Christians scorn the concept that it is possible to live a life in perfect harmony with the Savior. Young people, you cannot depend upon your experience-driven understandings. Many people have heard that victorious living is impossible. They have heard Christian teachers and preachers confidently affirm it to be so. They have sometimes read it in books, and they know that they personally are saying and doing things which are not Christ-like in nature. Above all, they witness other young people and other adults who claim to be Christians but who often show very un-Christ-like characteristics. Thus without any further question or study, they are content to live a faulted life, believing that somehow, someway, when Jesus returns they will be saved in His kingdom. The study of the Bible draws one to entirely different conclusions. We remember an American preacher, famous for his many books, visiting Australia, after preaching a divine service to a large college congregation in which he read no Bible verse, yet concluded with a benediction in which he prayed, "Thank You that You have not asked us to be perfect." The authors were stunned. It is true that God has not *asked* us to be perfect. While on earth Jesus *commanded* His people to be perfect.

Be ye therefore perfect, even as your Father which is in heaven is perfect.
Matthew 5:48

To most Christians this text is interpreted to mean "try to be perfect, but you never will be perfect." That exact mentality is brought into the marriage experience. In many contexts, marriage is frequently called a union. But a true union is built upon unity, that bond in which there is no area of separation between those united together. If young people would study the experience of Pentecost in Acts chapter two, they will reflect that about one hundred and twenty people were united.

And when the day of Pentecost was fully come, they were all with one accord in one place. Acts 2:1

Success in marriage is certainly a union built upon unity. The same agreement regarding divisive principles that brings unity in a group of Christian believers is necessry for unity in a marriage. Unity, however, does not mean that we always think exactly the same. However, it entails both spouses having their lives in unbroken commitment to their Savior, allowing Him to perfect His character in their lives. In His prayer for unity Jesus said,

Sanctify them through thy truth: thy word is truth. John 17:17

Paul's unity chapter addressed to the Ephesian believers provides the plain meaning of unity.

For the perfecting of the saints, for the work of the ministry, for the edifying of the body of Christ: Till we all come in the unity of the faith, and of the knowledge of the Son of God, unto a perfect man, unto the measure of the stature of the fulness of Christ: that we henceforth be no more children, tossed to and fro, and carried about with every wind of doctrine, by the sleight of men, and cunning craftiness, whereby they lie in wait to deceive; But speaking the truth in love, may grow up into him in all things, which is the head, even Christ
Ephesians 4:12–15

You will notice a number of key words in this beautiful passage such as, "perfecting of the saints," "unity of the faith," "perfect man," "stature of the fulness of Christ;" "speaking the truth in love." These represent the highest principles of unity. Such principles are also defined by Peter.

> Seeing ye have purified your souls in obeying the truth through the Spirit unto unfeigned love of the brethren, see that ye love one another with a pure heart fervently.   1 Peter 1:22

Here again we notice some principles which bring true unity—"have purified your souls;" "obeying the truth;" "through the [Holy] Spirit;" "unto unfeigned [without pretense] love of the brethren." Young people, can you see that these are the principles upon which every true Christian marriage should be established? You must understand that if both the husband and the wife are daily seeking, in the power of Christ's grace, to live this life, then the marriage will be invincible. Some believe that this is a noble goal but that it cannot be achieved. However, the Bible does not support such a discouraging conclusion. Some believe that Bible statements such as "I can of mine own self do nothing" (John 5:30) absolves them of any thought to seek perfection of character. Yet it is from Jesus that we are assured that "with God all things are possible" (Matthew 19:26). The issue of perfection has nothing to do with the abject weakness of fallen human beings. It has all to do with Christ dwelling with us.

> Let this mind be in you, which was also in Christ Jesus.   Philippians 2:5

> Whereby are given unto us exceeding great and precious promises: that by these ye might be partakers of the divine nature, having escaped the corruption that is in the world through lust.   2 Peter 1:4

If we say it is impossible to live a life of character perfection, we certainly will never achieve it. We understand that that is exactly the same principle which we see in what is said by so many husbands and wives about their marriage. They confess "There is no hope. We cannot learn how to agree and continue to live together." If you conclude this, you are expressing a self-fulfilling prophecy. As you allow your mind to wander in that direction you certainly will never find God's plan to bring about unity, love and harmony in your marriage. The more we express this hopelessness, the deeper its impression, for expressions inevitably deepen impressions. You become increasingly convinced of the impossibility of a happy and contented marriage. Thus step by step you yield to the temptation to fracture the marriage vows.

Long before marriage you must realize the infinite power of Christ and His grace, day by day and moment by moment, to provide you victory over the tests, trials and temptations of Satan. On numbers of occasions Christ provided the perfect formula. When Christ is in us and we are in Christ we are invincible to the fiery darts of Satan.

At that day ye shall know that I am in my Father, and ye in me; and I in you.

John 14:20

I am the vine, ye are the branches: He that abideth in me, and I in him, the same bringeth forth much fruit: for without me ye can do nothing. If a man abide not in me, he is cast forth as a branch, and is withered; and men gather them and cast them into the fire, and they are burned. If ye abide in me, and my words abide in you, ye shall ask what ye will, and it shall be done unto you.

John 15:5–7

Hereby know we that we dwell in him, and he in us, because he hath given us of his Spirit. . . . Whosoever shall confess that Jesus is the Son of God, God dwelleth in him, and he in God. And we have known and believed the love that God hath to us. God is love; and he that dwelleth in love dwelleth in God, and God in him.

1 John 4:13, 15–16

We abide in Christ when we have a living connection with Him and we renew it every morning on our knees. By submitting our lives to Him we can have the strength to live a loving, kind, patient and contented life. James very positively states,

Submit yourselves therefore to God. Resist the devil, and he will flee from you.

James 4:7

Both spouses must have that power of victory in their lives. Young people should patiently seek a marriage partner who also is gaining the same daily strength and victory. There is one thing certain: such a marriage will never suffer fracture. As the years of marriage pass into decades, the marriage bond will strengthen the love of both husband and wife for the other. The children of the marriage will have the joy of growing up in a home where they too experience the joy, the calmness, the blessing of such a Christian home. It is often said that it takes two to make a divorce. That is false. It only takes one to make a divorce, but it certainly takes two—two dedicated, mature Christians—to make an invincible marriage.

Young people, our motivation for writing this book is that you will be content with nothing less than such an invincible marriage.

7

"I DO"

"**I** DO." These two monosyllabic words comprise a total of three letters of the alphabet. The implications of these words in a marriage ceremony represent one of the most sacred utterances made by a human being. It is impossible to overestimate the importance of these two words, for they represent a pledge of allegiance, loyalty, fidelity, integrity, veracity, and honesty. Marriage vows are lifelong commitments. Therefore, to reach this stage of commitment to a member of the opposite sex, they should be undertaken only after the most dedicated, prayerful and studied preparation.

First and foremost, the one contemplating such a move needs to undertake the most earnest heartsearching to be sure that he or she, each one, is not being rash or precipitous in making such a commitment to another individual. The decision must not be made alone upon the physical attraction of the individual, nor upon the personality, education, the likelihood of being a very capable provider of the necessities or even the luxuries of life, or being potentially a person of prestige and honor in church and/or society. This decision must depend foremost upon one's own character, loyalty to God, willingness to undertake service to God and man, talent, and an experience which will enhance the ministry of the home as a witnessing citadel in the community. It should also take into account a ready preparedness for physical responsibility and compassionate care in the future for the parents of the other spouse. It is essential to have developed skills and commitment to solving difficulties in God's way. Further, there should be the quality of maturity to train and educate the children who might bless the marriage.

When Colin was president of a senior Christian college in the United States, the Assistant Dean of Women, at twenty-six years of age, with great expressions of happiness, revealed that she had just become engaged to marry a young man. In conversation with this Christian young lady, Colin asked her a little about the man, whom he had not met for he lived a thousand miles distant from the college. Colin had great admiration for this young lady, and knew that she was a woman who had given deep evidence that she was truly a faithful Christian. However, his interest increased even further when she added, "And *we* want you to perform our wedding." He knew this was the request of the young lady, but no doubt she had talked it over with her fiancé, who had agreed to her suggestion. Colin gave no direct response to the request to perform the wedding, but pointed out that he had not met the young man and would love to meet him. She responded, "Oh that will be possible soon because in two weeks time he will be visiting me." At that point Colin offered an invitation for them to share Friday evening supper at his house, which she eagerly accepted.

When the couple arrived, naturally, Colin's focus was especially upon the young man. Was this young man worthy of such a fine Christian woman? On the surface things went well. He was attractive physically, and very personable. He was a good conversationalist and an active worker in his local church. He had obtained his degree of Master in Business Administration. He had a fine future ahead of him and had already made good progress in the business world. However, when the conversation turned to spiritual matters Colin was quite surprised. Whereas the Assistant Dean of Women enthusiastically joined in the spiritual dialogue, her fiancé was strangely silent. No longer was he an active conversationalist as he had been when dialoguing upon more general themes.

This troubled Colin, and he was filled with mixed feelings when they left. He sensed the young man was not anywhere near exhibiting the spiritual dedication which the Assistant Dean of Women had many times witnessed to him. While it could not be said that this marriage would be the yoking together of unbelievers, nevertheless, there seemed to be a great spiritual divide between the two.

Colin contemplated the rest of the weekend what he believed to be a very unsatisfactory choice, and wondered what he could do to alert this young woman to the danger she was facing. He was very well aware that, often, talking directly to young ladies throws them into a defensive mode, and thereby all opportunity is lost to help them work through their thinking. In reality he did not have too much time to think. On Monday morning as Colin was outside his office, the Assistant Dean passed by and engaged Colin in dialogue concerning her fiancé. She asked him point blank what was his evaluation of her fiancé. What a difficult position Colin found himself in! With the help of the Lord he told the young woman all the positive characteristics that he had noted, but then, he believes under the promptings of the Holy Spirit, he asked a simple question, "Are there any areas where you do not see eye to eye, that need to be resolved before your marriage?"

She was surprisingly reticent to answer that question, but after an extended hesitation she said, "Well, I love animals and he does not want any animals in or around our home." Colin asked her, "Can you live with that?" She responded that she thought that would not be a great impediment to their marriage. Now Colin recognized the approach he should employ— periodic questions.

A few days later Colin met her again, and, once again the conversation turned to her fiancé. He reminded her of what she had said in the previous conversation concerning their differences on animals. Then he asked, "Are there any other issues which separate you at this point of time?" Once again there was an extended pause. This time, however, she raised a much more serious situation. She said, "Well, there is one thing that does trouble me. I do not want a television in our home, but he is almost addicted to television." This revelation startled Colin, and in response he asked, "What are you going to do about that?" She responded, "Well, if he wants a television, he will have to have it downstairs in the basement. I am determined not to have a television in the living areas of the home."

Colin persisted, "So you are going to be upstairs working or studying and he is going to be downstairs watching television. Is that really the kind of marriage for which you are hoping?" In a somber tone, she admitted that it was not. Colin continued, "Should God bless this union with children, what are you going to do about them?" "Oh, I would not permit them to watch television in the basement." He responded, "How realistic is that? Such a prohibition has the fundamental basis of a major disagreement, and bringing an area of stress into the marriage." Then Colin urged her seriously to find a resolution to this issue before the marriage.

By this time Colin was very unsure that he would agree to perform such a marriage. This was a serious, unresolved issue. While often the unmarried do not see the immensity of the consequences which can follow, nevertheless, it was his responsibility not to be part of a marriage which was sure to result in serious conflict, to present problems which could become big and bring great stress into that marriage, problems which could lead, if not to separation and divorce, at least to likelihood of fuelling arguments and disharmony in the marriage and lead to duplicity in the minds of the children.

Several days later the Assistant Dean and Colin, again, had opportunity to speak. Once again he asked, "Are there other issues you have not yet discussed with me where there is disagreement?" He was not ready for the response. She said, "Yes there is. After his visit to me, while we were waiting for the plane at the airport, I was shocked that he went to the magazine stands, took out a *Playboy Magazine* and started perusing it. Of course I protested to him." "What was his response?" questioned Colin. "Oh," he said, "I'm only interested in the art." Colin persisted, "Did you believe him?"

She made it plain that she did not believe his explanation. With great earnestness Colin said, "Is *that* the kind of marriage which you desire?" With somber and downcast appearance, so contrary to her normal buoyant and vibrant Christian experience, she responded in the negative.

It was only a few more days before Colin met her again. This time there was no buoyancy, no sparkle in the eye. Colin asked her if there was anything wrong. No response. Unexpectedly, she said, "Would you be hurt if you did not perform our wedding?" It gave a great degree of relief to Colin that she asked that question. He assured her that if they had found someone else they would rather have perform the wedding, it would not in any way hurt him. Indeed, Colin had made the decision that he would not perform the wedding, and knew that in the very near future he would have had to explain this to the Assistant Dean. However, she explained, "I have just broken my engagement. I cannot go ahead with this marriage." Colin did everything to affirm her, and while comforting her, he expressed the relief which he felt. Not only did he tell her that he had previously made the decision not to perform the wedding but that in the broadest sense of Scripture, he believed they would be unequally yoked together had they married.

It took courage at that late stage, but it was the only proper decision to make. It was sad that the romance had progressed to the point that it had before that decision was made. Yet it was much better never to reach the altar and say "I Do," and then be bound by a sacred vow to a man who did not share the same spiritual values or the same moral integrity.

This is why great care must be taken before entering into a courtship. It cannot be "love at first sight." It cannot be a quick infatuation. Marriage represents one of the highest principles of this planet.

Especially in this age when divorce is epidemic, and the misery and unhappiness which attends it is so great, long contemplation should be taken, by both the young man and the young woman, before even reaching the point where they would consider exploring a courtship. Both must be frank, open, and honest with each other so that the values, principles, and direction of the life calling can be well evaluated. There should not be the slightest thought, "Well, in the marriage I can help change him or her." It would certainly be preferable never to be married than to end with an unhappy marriage which would destroy the lives of children and the blessings of a home.

We earnestly entreat all young people to keep in mind the solemnity of marriage and the vow "I do" which is such a solemn commitment and which impacts mightily upon the future of the individuals in this life and in the life hereafter.

8

Counsel to Parents

IT is true that parents cannot be held responsible for everything their children do. Nevertheless, they play a primary role in the life patterns of their children. It is rare, when the decision is made to seek to have a child, that married couples do much thinking concerning the future life experience which they desire for that child. Even when the child is an infant or is reaching towards his teens, rarely is considered thought given to the preparation of the child for marriage and adult responsibilities. At every step along the child's life journey, parents need to consider their philosophy of child training not only for the immediate needs of the child, but also they must exercise long sight, looking ahead to the mature decisions which they desire their children to make in their teenage years and adulthood. The children will be greatly affected by the training which they receive in their homes from infancy upward.

In the broadest principles of training, children do best in homes where the parents have fair but firm parameters which are applied consistently and persistently by both parents. Erratic parents, who themselves are undisciplined, inevitably provide erratic environments where the child cannot predict the parental response to particular behaviors. This frequently results in instability and insecurity when the child reaches adolescence. The training of a child in selflessness is also a foundational pillar of balanced maturity in later life.

The compelling influence of peer group pressure is sufficient for every responsible parent to guard carefully, not only the friendships which they permit, but also the chaperonage by the adults of a mixed group of young people including their children. We are not confining our comments to boy-girl friendships. Young people, especially boys, sometimes resort to serious mischief when they are together which they would not do alone. If your child is inclined to be a follower, the dangers are even greater. However, if your child is a leader and you know that he is far from being converted, he may lead another child into activities which have serious negative consequences. Many a teenager's life is blighted, and sometimes forfeited, by youthful associations.

Parents who permit early dating are irresponsible. That many other parents allow early dating is no justification for a Christian to follow the pathway of the majority. Our decisions are not based upon what fallible and often unconverted parents do; they are based upon the principles of the sacred Word of God and the tragic results of permissive society. If not properly instructed throughout their lives, children almost inevitably move into pathways which greatly threaten their future happiness, and certainly parents will be responsible for a greatly diminished likelihood that their children will follow the life of Christ.

Parents have to be prepared to resist pressure from their children. Parents often have pressure exerted upon them to break down the principles of God. Children frequently pit their parents against the more liberal and laissez-faire parents of their friends. Many professed Christian parents show great weakness under such pressure. We well remember the pressure we placed upon our parents, especially our mother, when we were teenagers. It was true that other children in the same church which we attended were given significantly more "privileges" than our parents permitted us. Today we are deeply thankful that our parents did not yield to the pressure we attempted to assert upon them by comparing them unfavorably with the parents of other children in our church.

Of course, the firmness of the parents is so much more effective if there is no outburst of emotion but just firm, unwavering, wise decisions. Children must know that their parents do not yield to pressure, not because they delight to make things tough for the children, but rather it is because they love them dearly and are prepared to take these stands to protect the children from situations which will be destructive of their happiness now, and certainly threatening to their stability in the future.

Young people who do not engage in what some call "puppy love," a term which sounds rather innocent but can prove deadly dangerous, have a much greater likelihood of making careful and wise decisions in the choice of a marriage partner. Children barely into their teens, as well as those in their late teens, are not mature enough, and certainly are not sufficiently developed in their spiritual values, to make wise judgments in the choice of a marriage partner.

Children who grow up in a quality Christian home where their parents provide a secure, happy home, and show the joy there is in worshiping and serving God, and train their children from an early age to be a blessing to others and to reach out in witness for their Savior, are most likely to establish a strong Christian home. There are many rewarding things which children can achieve as they witness for the Lord. The least a family with children can do is to visit regularly a nursing home. Elderly people generally love to have children and young people visit them. Even small children can play a role, perhaps singing with their parents or reciting a text of scripture. Small children also can help distribute Christian literature. Children can participate in sharing gifts with needy people, and perhaps painting or drawing or making little gifts themselves to present to those who are underprivileged. They may help to do housework or yard work for the sick and the elderly.

Parents who themselves are very creative, can find many other ways to train their children to reach out to others. These become excellent family activities which, rather than being self-serving activities, teach the children how to be happy helping others. In such training the parents are developing a love for selfless activity and the rewards which will come from helping others. These activities are secure foundations for a happy marriage. While every child ultimately has to make his own decision and commitment to the Lord, nevertheless, parents have the privilege of providing a firm foundation from which those decisions can be made. The wise man said,

> Train up a child in the way he should go: and when he is old, he will not depart from it.   Proverbs 22:6

9

Carefully and Wisely

THE wise man, King Solomon, under inspiration of God, has given young men much counsel when considering a wife. This counsel has stood the test of time. The age in which we live is just as needful of this counsel as the days in which Solomon wrote the book of Proverbs. We will begin with Solomon's general counsel,

Whoso findeth a wife findeth a good thing, and obtaineth favour of the Lord.
Proverbs 18:22

If Christian young men were to consult this counsel of Solomon alone, it may seem that any woman who is chosen as a wife would lead the husband to receive the approbation, praise and approval of God. Certainly it is in the plan of God that men, at the appropriate time of life, will take unto them a woman as their wife and companion in life; each one complementing the other in the Christian walk and in the training of any children that might bless the marriage. Solomon did not limit his general counsel to young men. In many statements he is very specific concerning the characteristics of a wife, appropriate for a God-fearing young man.

. . . a prudent wife is from the Lord.
Proverbs 19:14

The word "prudent" means "planning carefully ahead of time; sensible; discreet" (Thorndike-Barnhart Comprehensive Desk Dictionary, Doubleday & Company, Inc., Garden City, New York, 1955).

It will take time for a man to consider the virtues of a young lady. A prudent woman will not speak before she thinks; she will not be rash in making judgments; she will hear both sides of a story before coming to conclusions; she will learn that there are many things which are best left unsaid; she will use finances carefully; she will follow God's Word; she will never speak negatively about her husband nor her children; she will be a wise counselor; she will be punctual; she will never be boastful of power; she will consider the health of her husband and children in the preparation of food; she will give wise, loving counsel to her children; and she will train up the children in the ways of the Lord.

Very important is Solomon's counsel, which is recorded at the end of the book of Proverbs, concerning the choice of a wife.

> Who can find a virtuous woman? For her price is far above rubies. The heart of her husband doth safely trust in her, so that he shall have no need of spoil. [12] She will do him good and not evil all the days of her life. She seeketh wool, and flax, and worketh willingly with her hands. She is like the merchants' ships; she bringeth her food from afar. She riseth also, while it is yet night, and giveth meat to her household, and a portion to her maidens. She considereth a field, and buyeth it: with the fruit of her hands she planteth a vineyard. She girdeth her loins with strength, and strengtheneth her arms. She perceiveth that her merchandise is good: her candle goeth not out by night. She layeth her hands to the spindle, and her hands hold the distaff. She stretcheth out her hand to the poor; yea, she reacheth forth her hands to the needy. She is not afraid of the snow for her household: for all her household are clothed with scarlet. She maketh herself coverings of tapestry, her clothing is silk and purple. Her husband is known in the gates, when he sitteth among the elders of the land. She maketh fine linen, and selleth it; and delivereth girdles unto the merchants. Strength and honour are her clothing; and she shall rejoice in time to come. She openeth her mouth with wisdom; and in her tongue is the law of kindness. She looketh well to the ways of her household, and eateth not the bread of idleness. Her children arise up, and call her blessed; her husband also, and he praiseth her. Many daughters have done virtuously, but thou excellest them all. Favour is deceitful, and beauty is vain; but a woman that feareth the Lord, she shall be praised. Give her of the fruit of her hands; and let her own works praise her in the gate.   Proverbs 31:10–31

Look deeply into this counsel. Verse 10, *a virtuous woman*. A virtuous woman is a woman of highest moral integrity; a woman who has kept herself from yielding to seduction; has honored God by living a life of purity and integrity; a woman who has not yielded to customs or to the low immorality of carnally minded men, a young woman whose integrity is inviolate.

Verse 11, *the heart of her husband doth safely trust in her.* A woman who before marriage has lived a virtuous life is a woman whom her husband can safely trust. There will be no need to suspect that she will cast her eyes in the direction of another man. She is a woman who is wholly directed by the Holy Spirit so that she will avoid evil in her future. Thus she will do good all the days of her life. She is wholly committed to the lifelong partnership with her husband. She will not contemplate separation or divorce; she will not undermine other people's confidence in her husband; she will stand by him and with him no matter what the vicissitudes of life might be.

Verse 13, . . . *worketh willingly with her hands.* A good wife will be industrious, there will not be a lazy bone in her body. She will see the importance of time and the usefulness that must be exercised in the use of time. She will be diligent to do all that is necessary to keep the house clean, to prepare the clothes necessary for her husband and children, to spend time in the training of her children. Too, she will be employed not only in the home but, if possible, in the garden. She will employ some of her time in missionary endeavor and in the care of the needy, and will train her children in such activities.

Verse 14, . . . *bringeth her food from afar.* This is a reference to finding the best food to place on the table for her family if she lives in a country in which it is difficult to grow a wide variety of foods. She will provide nutritious food for her family.

Verse 15, . . . *giveth meat to her household.* She arises from bed before the break of day preparing food for breakfast. This indicates that she understands the importance of the first meal of the day. Often the first meal is not the most carefully prepared meal, though it should be the main meal of the day. It is much easier today, with our refrigeration units and our heating units, to prepare the food ahead of time for the morning. It was not so in Solomon's time, when a fire had to be lit and food prepared the same morning. Nevertheless, the principle remains that she will take care of a good, nutritious breakfast for the family. Not least, she trains her children in these habits.

Verse 16, . . . *planteth a vineyard.* This is a woman who does not consider simply doing her housework, but she cultivates the land and no doubt uses it as a training place for her children. Thus much of the food which the family eats will be freshly grown with the best of gardening principles. As far as possible she will avoid the use of inorganic fertilizers, herbicides and pesticides, and will avoid genetically engineered foods.

Verse 17, . . . *She girdeth her loins with strength, and strengtheneth her arms.* The wife is a woman who obtains her exercise in the physical work she accomplishes. Further she wears the kind of clothing best suited to the climate, and appropriate for her activities.

Verse 18, *She perceiveth that her merchandise is good.* This wife chooses wisely everything which she purchases, seeking to buy the best value for her money. It may not be the least expensive, but it may be the most enduring and of the best quality that she can afford both for herself and family.

Verse 19, *She layeth her hands to the spindle.* This is another indication of the industry of this wife. She does not occupy her days in meaningless viewing of television programs, surfing the Internet, reading unprofitable magazines and books, but she is occupying her time with that which would be a blessing to her and her family and honors the Lord.

Verse 20, *She stretcheth out her hand to the poor.* This is a woman who is compassionate. Mindful of the needs of her family, she also sees her responsibility to help those who are genuinely poor. Such a woman will be wise. She will not support the lazy and indolent who should supply for themselves. She will work to do her best to help those who are suffering, the poor, the sick and the aged.

Verse 21, *She is not afraid of the snow for her household.* This is because she has her family thoroughly and appropriately clothed for such winter conditions. It was the practice of her day to dress appropriately for the climatic conditions.

Verse 22, *She maketh . . . clothing,* Women today in the western world often have not learned the skill of making their own clothing. This lack makes very difficult the choice of modest apparel, inasmuch as most clothing is riveted upon fashion, often unsuitable for a Christian.

Verse 23, *Her husband . . . sitteth among the elders of the land.* This woman has not accepted the invitation of a man who does not have the qualities of leadership, for she knows that such men are not likely to make suitable husbands and fathers because they are weak, and she has waited until a man of high integrity and capabilities has invited her to share her life with him.

Verse 24, *She maketh fine linen, and selleth it.* Here is a woman who, if necessary, has a home industry which can add to the income of the family to provide the necessities of life, to have funds to share with the work of God and to help the needy. She is obviously too prudent to use the family income for selfish goals and indulgences.

Verse 25, *Strength and honour are her clothing.* This woman is an emotionally strong and stable individual, not given to moodiness nor to bursts of frivolity, a woman who is honored by her relatives, her neighbors, her friends and by her fellow church members.

Verse 26, *She openeth her mouth with wisdom; and . . . the law of kindness.* This woman has a wonderful combination, wise words delivered in kindness. What a fine wife such a lady is! What a treasure she is to a godly husband!

Verse 27, *. . . eateth not the bread of idleness.* It has been strongly emphasized in the previous verses that this woman is productive, and at the end of the day she can see that she has accomplished much and honored the Lord.

Verse 28, *Her children . . . call her blessed; her husband also.* This woman has earned the trust, the respect and the love of all the members of the family. The children have had a model for their lives which has attracted them to exemplify the same principles.

Verse 29, *Many daughters have done virtuously, but thou excellest them all.* This lady fulfills the characteristics of the very best wives and mothers. A godly husband will not seek for someone else but will thank God for such a wonderful companion with whom to share life's experience. Wisely and confidently she is preparing to be part of all those whose names will be written in the book of life. She will share eternity with all others who have been faithful to the Savior.

Verse 30, *. . . woman that feareth the Lord.* This verse brings us back to the qualities presented in verses twelve and thirteen. This woman follows in all the ways of God. She loves and serves God with all her heart and soul. She keeps His commandments and His statutes. (See Deuteronomy 10:12, 13).

Verse 31, *. . . let her own works praise her.* This is a woman who does not have to sing her own praises, does not wear a false pride. Her works lead to praise, not because she is seeking it, but because her life is exemplary.

How thankful we are for the wise counsel of Solomon. Some young men may say such a woman does not exist. Granted that few such women exist, but such a sweetheart is the one for whom wise young men will wait. They do exist. They are to be found. They are to be sought out, but only by those who themselves are just as praiseworthy. We earnestly counsel godly men to settle for nothing less than such a woman with whom to share your life, one who can be trusted to be a godly mother of your children.

10
Consequences of Choosing the Wrong Wife

Y OUNG men, though committed to the Savior in so many ways, do not always show great wisdom in choosing their life partner. They often permit physical attractions or personality characteristics to dominate their decision making. So often they seek ways to be able to lead the one to whom they are attracted in the right paths once they are married. How unwise is the assumption that after marriage the character of the spouse will be transformed, although under rare circumstances this may take place. This optimistic course is too risky and fraught with perilous dangers to pursue. Rarely are the hopes of such a husband realized. This leads to great anguish and frustration, and children initiated into the family are placed in spiritual danger. The divided loyalties, the inconsistencies, sad to say, lead many children to follow the ways of the unconverted parent. This is especially true when the mother is the unconverted parent, because mothers almost inevitably build a stronger influence over the children than the father.

If any young man is in the process of making a decision concerning marriage to such an unconverted young lady, this is the time to redress that situation. Painful though it may be, the pain of a lifetime will be vastly worse and too many lives will be involved in the negative consequences. If the children ultimately go astray they will lead their children in the ways of Satan also, and so the effects have no stopping point. The young suitor is imperiling his future grandchildren. Few ever look down the corridor of the future to consider the consequences.

The pain of separating now will be much less than the constant pain which comes decade after decade in a marriage. Young men, seek out the counsel of godly adults. Ask them to help you to make the right decision. Ask them to be plain with you and not to hold back their evaluation, for truly much is at stake. Keep in mind that the Lord has paramount claims upon your life and service. God has called each one to His service.

You may think it preposterous to compare modern man with some of the greatest prophets of all time. Yet today God is raising up men to be the spiritual giants around the world. It is obvious that God has called each one of us from before we were born. He holds the right to expect all of us to fulfill His calling upon our lives and service. How few ever achieve the fullness of God's ambitions for them. Let us briefly review such men of the Bible.

First let us direct our attention to John the Baptist. Jesus said there was no greater prophet than John.

> Verily I say unto you, Among them that are born of women there hath not risen a greater than John the Baptist.   Matthew 11:11

The Scripture also instructs us that he was endowed with the Holy Ghost before birth.

> . . . he shall be filled with the Holy Ghost, even from his mother's womb.
>   Luke 1:15

The reason why John could be filled with the Holy Ghost from his mother's womb was because his mother was filled with the Holy Ghost.

> . . . and Elisabeth was filled with the Holy Ghost.   Luke 1:41

And he was brought up with a father who also was filled with the Holy Ghost.

> And his father Zacharias was filled with the Holy Ghost.   Luke 1:67

Godly, Spirit-filled men must marry Spirit-filled women to provide a Spirit-filled home. God has chosen the most trustworthy men to be leaders to give the everlasting gospel to the world, and most of them will have been raised in such homes. It is not to exclude others who did not grow up in such homes; however, how much more certain it will be if godly men marry godly women to parent such a generation.

We cannot forget the words of the prophet Isaiah.

> Listen, O isles, unto me; and hearken, ye people, from far; The Lord hath called me from the womb; from the bowels of my mother hath he made mention of my name.   Isaiah 49:1

God has not revealed many details concerning the background of Isaiah. Yet we know that he was the son of Amoz, most probably not a prominent man in Judah. The name of his mother is hid from us; but of one thing we can be sure: he grew up in a godly family. That is why Isaiah could say that he had been called from the womb. Of course he could not understand this call when he was a fetus in the womb of his mother nor during his early life as he grew up. However, under the guidance of godly parents, no doubt there became increasingly clear to him the nature of the divine calling which God had placed upon his life and service—not a life of ease, nor of popularity. Indeed yours could well be a life of great persecution and may lead to martyrdom. What a prophet Isaiah was! Often he is called the "gospel prophet" because of his prophecies about Jesus. He was greatly persecuted, despised and ultimately martyred.

Come to Jeremiah. Here we have the words of God Himself.

> Before I formed thee in the belly, I knew thee and before thou camest forth out of the womb I sanctified thee, and I ordained thee a prophet unto the nations.
>
> Jeremiah 1:5

God made it plain that He knew Jeremiah before he was conceived. He too was sanctified before he was born. A little more information is known concerning Jeremiah's father than Isaiah's father. Hilkiah, Jeremiah's father, was a priest, as was John the Baptist's father, Zacharias. There is no mention of his mother's name but there is no way that he could have been sanctified in the womb of his mother unless she was under the guidance of the Holy Spirit. The calling and ordination came before he was born. That is true of all young men and young women. The Bible makes it plain that the blueprint of every one of us is recorded perfectly in heaven. The individuality which we possess is recorded in the books of heaven.

> For thou hast possessed my reins: thou hast covered me in my mother's womb. I will praise thee; for I am fearfully and wonderfully made: marvelous are thy works; and that my soul knoweth right well. My substance was not hid from thee, when I was made in secret, and curiously wrought in the lowest parts of the earth. Thine eyes did see my substance, yet being unperfect; and in thy book all my members were written, which in continuance were fashioned, when as yet there was none of them.
>
> Psalm 139:13–16

A man should not marry until he has determined the calling which Christ has placed upon him and until he has responded to that calling and will have undertaken necessary training for that calling. Then wisely he will seek a wife who will be a complement to his calling. It would be a sad marriage if even two fully dedicated young people were to marry whose callings were incompatible with one another. This sometimes happens.

Colin was a member of a committee which appointed pastors to various districts in an east coast conference of the United States. The time had come for a pastor to be transferred to another district. The committee faced a very difficult situation. He had a wife, a godly woman, and in many ways a very fine wife. However there was one problem. She was a physician. She had built up a very successful practice in the city in which they lived and where he had been serving. In the end he decided that he could not move from that city because of the profession of his wife. I am not suggesting in any way that God cast off either of these spouses. I had no doubt however that the husband's ministry had been compromised, and though he carried on some functions for the church, he never again was to serve in the full role of a pastor.

We occasionally have spoken to young people who have evaluated that these standards are so high they will never find a suitable wife. Young people, you do not have to find a wife. Yet we are not suggesting that you do not seek a life partner, but that search begins down on your knees. You are asking the Lord to lead and guide you, to give you mature wisdom well above your years, guided by older people who discern godly young men and young women. God knows where your future wife is. He knows how to put you in touch with such a one at the appropriate time. Remember, a poor choice of a wife can greatly diminish the effectiveness of your ministry and mission for the Lord. The wrong choice of a wife can ruin the influence of her husband. Even if she does not ruin his influence, she can cause great anguish throughout life.

You can see examples of this in the Bible. King Ahab ignored the virtuous women in the kingdom of Israel and sought a wife among the pagans in Zidon. He chose to marry the daughter of Ethbaal, the king of Zidon—a wicked pagan woman named Jezebel. Because of her, Ahab raised up an altar to Baal (1 Kings 16:31, 32). No doubt it was because Ahab himself was an unconverted man that he chose such an evil wife. Yet there can be no question that the evils of King Ahab were greatly enhanced by the influence of this pagan, wicked queen whom he had married.

Review the record of Samson, who was directly called of God to be a prophet in his day, and his tragic decision to ignore his parents' counsel and marry a woman of the Philistines. We will never know on this earth, and may never know at all, depending upon God's wisdom, what that prophet would have achieved had he married a godly woman from his own nation. We know, too, that his life and therefore his ministry was greatly shortened, because of the decision which he had made to marry the wrong woman. Samson placed beauty of face and body before beauty of heart. Read the divine account of his courtship,

> And Samson went down to Timnath, and saw a woman in Timnath of the daughters of the Philistines. And he came up, and told his father and his mother, and said, I have seen a woman in Timnath of the daughters of the Philistines: now therefore get her for me to wife. Then his father and his mother said unto him, Is there never a woman among the daughters of thy brethren, or among all my people, that thou goest to take a wife of the uncircumcised Philistines? And Samson said unto his father, Get her for me; for she pleaseth me well.
>
> Judges 14:1–3

In more recent history, one of the greatest and most admired Protestant Reformers, John Wesley, seemed to have very poor judgment in his direction in seeking a wife. He created great problems for himself in America when suddenly he broke off a relationship with a young American woman, causing him to lose credibility and hastening his return to Great Britain probably long before it was God's plan. When he did marry, he chose a woman who evidenced only un-Christlike characteristics—a woman who made life miserable for him. Though he was faithful to her, she brought constant grief to his life. How sad that he could not have married a true "helpmeet."

A poor marriage partner can lead to financial difficulties for the husband, even causing him to fall into great debt, taking his time from the ministry to which God has called him. Some men have been compelled to resile from the work of the Lord in order to seek a secular job affording high remuneration in order to meet the escalating debts of his spendthrift wife.

We emphasize again that after the decision to serve Christ, no other decision can affect the future of a young man more than the choice of a life partner. Wives so often become "the power behind the throne" and a godly wife can become a sanctifying influence to her husband. Contrariwise an ungodly wife can lead a man into making very poor decisions, which undermine the leadership responsibilities of that man. A wrong marriage can lead to lifelong bondage, for the clouds hang over the house constantly.

Seek earnestly and prayerfully to make objective decisions; remember the ancient proverb, "More haste, less speed." Take time to carefully weigh the issues. Will this young lady be a blessing and a helpmeet to enhance the calling that God has placed upon you, or will she in any way be a hindrance to your God-ordained ministry? Above everything else, a young man must seek to be assured that God has given His approval to such a marriage. Too much is at stake to risk anything less than an appropriate, careful choosing of the one who will helpfully and even cheerfully share the vicissitudes of life with you.

11

Qualities to Look For in a Future Husband

IF a man seeks your hand in marriage do not be flattered. It is essential that a young lady be wary of the overtures of a young man, especially if she knows but little of this man. Colin, from the time when he was President of West Indies College, recalls the wisdom of a young graduate. She had grown up in a home where her father was not a practicing Christian. She had accepted an invitation to serve the Lord in another country than Jamaica, her homeland. Not long after she had taken up her calling, a man, obviously attracted to her, sought to commence a friendship. Wisely she refused, stating that she hardly knew the man and that she would make no decisions until she had wise counsel concerning him. Of course this young man wondered how he could meet this criterion to begin a friendship with the young lady. After all she was in new country and had very few people whom she knew there to guide her. As he explored his dilemma with this young lady, she told him that she would not consider any courtship until he had "spent time with Dr. Standish," and he had given his evaluation to her. This created a further dilemma.

While serving in the West Indies, Colin had visited this young man's nation but there was no guarantee that he would again be there in the foreseeable future. It was not that this young lady did not see some good characteristics in this young man, but she had learned the wisdom of receiving wise counsel from those of experience. She had spent quite a deal of time in Colin's home as a student at the college and had gathered confidence in Colin and his wife, Cheryl. With this in mind she wrote to Colin and asked if any time in the near future he would be in that country. Colin had had no such immediate plans. However, he and his wife were traveling to Mexico to participate in meetings. Talking the request over with Cheryl, they decided that when they returned from Mexico they would travel via this country, meet this young man, spend time with him, evaluate his qualities, and then make the requested recommendation. Colin took this responsibility very seriously and prayerfully because he knew the future of these two young people was at stake. The young man agreed to this plan to spend time with Colin, although he had not met him. The young lady gave him no alternative. Colin spent a considerable time dialoguing, asking him questions, finding out more information concerning his own spiritual goals and his Christian commitment and service for the Lord. It did not take too long for Colin to realize that this young man had many very fine Christian characteristics. He was a man of considerable talent and intellect, possessing a strong commitment to his Savior and to the work of the Lord. Indeed, it was these characteristics that attracted him to this young lady. Not only was she an attractive young lady, but she had dedicated her life to the service of the Lord.

After their dialogue together Colin felt that he had found a new friend, and the rest is history. This couple have now been married for over thirty years and a good marriage it has been. They are the parents of two grown sons, both of whom have been brought up in the fear of the Lord. This couple have been Colin's and Cheryl's friends ever since. Colin was thankful to the Lord that He gave him the right advice, because it is a very solemn responsibility to know that one's decision can break or make a marriage. The wisdom of this young lady was an example to all consecrated young ladies. Young ladies, take seriously your obligation to God to marry men who have Christian integrity and deep commitment to Christ and His service.

Christian men and women of experience will often be given wisdom to discern the character of young people, and their readiness to explore a romance and to consider the prospect of courtship. This young lady was very wise. She did not decide to enter into the courtship until she had sufficient evidence and guidance to decide whether or not the exploration was wise. She was sufficiently mature to have completed her training for the Lord. Do not be swept off your feet by a charming man who may not hold the virtues which you desire in a future companion.

What are some of the characteristics which a young lady should look for in a young man?

1.   First and foremost, a young lady should know a man well enough to understand what his past life has been. Is he one who gives evidence of nobility of character, purity of life, and a man who is considerate and caring and thus worthy of consideration? Again we emphasize that a woman must be most careful not to entertain the thought that a man who is defective in these qualities is sure to improve after marriage. It is our experience that such a man, unless he is truly converted, will indeed develop even less noble characteristics after marriage.

2.   Does he have Christian maturity beyond his years and exhibit a serious approach to all important matters of life?

3.   Is this man known for his modesty, simplicity and deep sincerity? Is he a young man who does not brag about his achievements or exploits?

4.   Is he a man who has a calm and even disposition? Does he show consideration? Does he address issues with appropriate objectivity?

5.   Does he have the respect of other men both young and old?

6.   How does he treat his mother? Does he show obvious love for her? Does he seek to please her and to honor her counsel? Is he solicitous of her comfort and quick to help her? Remember, the way he treats his mother and other ladies in his family, including his sisters, will have a profound influence upon his respect and genuine care for you.

7.   Is he free from self-centeredness, from carelessness in his habits? Does he seek to reduce the burdens which others have to bear and is he quick to notice how he can help his fellow human beings?

8.   How does he relate to the elderly? Does he treat them with kindness, respecting their age and their experience, unlike so many other young people who tend to ignore or make fun of their infirmities and weakness?

9.   Does he consistently practice reverence when in the house of the Lord or in the place of worship? Does he worship God, follow His Word and respect His ministers and elders?

10.   Does he have his private devotions morning and evening and does he also attend the family worship morning and evening if they are provided by his parents?

11.   Does he have a high desire to be at the worship meetings of the church? Is he attentive to what is taking place and not just there to be in your company?

12.   Is he a man of moral self-control and consecrated by the power of Jesus?

13.   What kind of books does he read? To what kind of programs does he listen?

14.   Does he show an interest in witnessing his love of Jesus with others and does he show an interest in helping the needy?

15.   Is he sober minded as Peter admonished the youth of his day?

> Be sober, be vigilant; because your adversary the devil, as a roaring lion, walketh about, seeking whom he may devour.   1 Peter 5:8

16.   Does he avoid the frivolity and carelessness of so many youth around him?

17. Is he a young man who can resist the wrong patterns of his peers and rather seek to lead them away from any activity which is inconsistent with the development of a true Christian character?

18. Are his words free from rudeness, coarseness and slang; does he show wisdom above his years? In other words, does he, in words and actions, show that he has surrendered his life to the Lord?

19. Is he kind, tenderhearted, long-suffering, forgiving and compassionate, seeking to avoid speaking evil of others but esteeming others better than himself?

> . . . in lowliness of mind let each esteem other[s] better than themselves (Philippians 2:3).

20. Is he attracted to you far more because of your character and your Christ-like virtues than your physical characteristics?

21. Is he careful with the finances which God has entrusted to him, responsible with assets, simple in his desires seeking to fulfill the necessities of life without extravagance or carelessness? Is he an energetic worker in his occupation and around the home and its grounds?

22. Does he avoid miserliness and would he be a man who would meet the necessary needs of his wife? Is he generous, indeed sacrificial, in helping the work of the Lord and the spread of the gospel, as well as providing help for any needy soul?

23. Is he a man who will allow your individuality to express your beliefs, convictions and opinions?

24. Would he permit you to have equal say in the important matters of dialogue? Is he solicitous of your counsel? Does he show evidence as seeing marriage as a partnership rather than a lordship?

25. Is he free from pride and personal ambition, and do his goals point to his desire to follow the calling of his Savior, irrespective of where it leads or into what field of endeavor it may take him, even if it brings deep sacrifice in his faithful service to God and man?

26. Is he sincere, free from deceit, free from saying one thing in front of a person and an altogether different thing behind that one's back?

27. Does he have a sensitive conscience, quick to ask forgiveness if it is necessary and to apologize for anything that might have been said or done out of place? Is he a gentle man, showing the Christian graces without false modesty?

28.   Is he free from an overbearing disposition, a man who is willing to be patient with any weakness which you have or mistakes that you make, while also seeking to help you to overcome these?

29.   Is he industrious, conscientious in the duties he is asked to fulfill even when there is no supervision of his work? Does he have a range of practical skills which will be valuable in his role as a husband and in the needs of the home?

30.   Does he love children? Will he be a wise father of any children which the Lord brings into your family should you marry him? Is he a man who will influence his children for good? Will he have patience and godly discipline without indulgence of his children?.

31.   Does he seek time with your parents and seek to get to know them, avoiding any attempt to take you away from them so that you can have more time alone? Do your parents find him to be a young man to whom they can entrust their beloved daughter to be a blessing and a help to her?

32.   What are his habits of dress, eating and drinking? Are they consistent with those of Biblical principles?

33.   What does he do in his discretionary time? Does he seek to do those things which are profitable, useful, and constructive rather than to waste his time on sports, worldly entertainment, indolence and frivolity? If his possesses a computer does he avoid addiction to it, using it only for appropriate and useful purposes, and does he limit the amount of time he spends with it?

34.   Is he emotionally stable, not easily ruffled in trying situations, free from violent outbursts, not holding anger, bitterness, hostility or revenge in his heart?

35.   Does he avoid lengthy pondering over negative situations which affect the work which God has called him to accomplish?

36.   Does he make quick and firm, but not rash, decisions?

37.   Make sure that he is a man who has avoided simply being "in love with love." Be certain that you are not just the latest fascination which he has developed.

38.   Does he have good physical health, live a temperate life, and have good physical strength?

39.   Does he avoid indulging himself with late nights, seeking to gain adequate rest nightly? Is he regularly up early to commune with God?

We understand that many of the young ladies may say such a young man does not exist. We hear godly young women asking the question, "Where can we find a godly young man whom we could trust as our life partner?" Almost as commonly we find godly young men asking similar questions. There are godly young men and women in this world; scarce they may be, but they can be found. God knows where they are. God knows the man or woman who is His choice for you as a life partner. If ever there is a matter to be placed before our Savior, it is the matter of the choice of a life partner. Remember the wonderful promise of Scripture,

> But seek ye first the kingdom of God, and his righteousness; and all these things shall be added unto you.   Matthew 6:33

We firmly believe that this promise, among many other things, applies to the finding of a life partner. God's timing knows no haste nor delay. It will be a timing perfect for you and when you meet or discover such a young man, God will guide and bring you together. His Word cannot fail. Trust Him.

12

The Youthful Lusts

MANY people, especially young men, have to confront the issue of masturbation. Misunderstanding and misinformation shadow this sensitive and often secretive issue. This is a scourge to almost every young man and a large number of young women. Some, especially males, recognizing the near-universality of the act, are inclined to think there is nothing wrong with it. However, this is not the case.

Paul, in his last letter in Scripture, had this to say,

> Flee also youthful lusts: but follow righteousness, faith, charity, peace, with them that call on the Lord out of a pure heart.   2 Timothy 2:22

Almost certainly among the youthful lusts Paul was referring to here is this issue of masturbation. He provided important counsel dealing with this grave addiction which plagues many youth. The advice he offers is: (1) follow righteousness, (2) exercise faith, (3) have charity or sincere God-like love, (4) be peaceable to others, and (5) above all, keep a pure heart.

> If a man therefore purge himself from these, he shall be a vessel unto honour, sanctified, and meet for the master's use, and prepared unto every good work.
> 2 Timothy 2:21

The purging of our heart from all iniquity is a daily need if we are to achieve the sanctification and honor which God has called each one of us to achieve. This is not the only time that Paul mentioned the situation to his young companion in labor for the Lord.

> But they that will be rich fall into temptation and a snare, and into many foolish and hurtful lusts, which drown men in destruction and perdition.
> 1 Timothy 6:9

To fail to follow these counsels will lead to destruction and perdition. Such purity is not only for our eternal life with the Lord but it is to be achieved now. Writing to another companion in labor, Titus, Paul stated,

> Teaching us that, denying ungodliness and worldly lusts, we should live soberly, righteously, and godly, in this present world.   Titus 2:12

 Peter and John also offer important counsel and warning against the lust of the flesh.

> Dearly beloved, I beseech you as strangers and pilgrims, abstain from fleshly lusts, which war against the soul.   1 Peter 2:11

Peter emphasized that such lusts war against our spiritual life, and we cannot have pure souls if we are given over to constant indulgence of the temptations of lust. John, in a very pointed way, shows that lust is inconsistent with the kingdom of heaven and to the righteousness of Christ, coming, as it does, directly from the perversion of the world.

> For all that is in the world, the lust of the flesh, and the lust of the eyes, and the pride of life, is not of the Father, but is of the world.   1 John 2:16

The words of Jesus Himself make it plain that lust, when cherished, is adultery.

> But I say unto you, That whosoever looketh on a woman to lust after her hath committed adultery with her already in his heart.   Matthew 5:28

It is certainly accurate to state that the basis of masturbation is a cherished lust which is sin. It is the lower nature, the carnal nature, which wars against ourselves. Lust is allowed to consume when we do not, in the power of Christ, guard jealously the avenues of the soul. Young people have a God-given responsibility to seek to avoid everything that would stimulate such evil thoughts. If conversations of other young people are moving in suggestive ways it is important to leave that conversation quickly. If material comes to us in any form, whether it be through any avenue of the media or signposts, we must quickly turn away from it. Even when we see a provocatively dressed young lady, young men are not to linger their eyes upon such a temptress, immediately asking God to protect them from these lustful thoughts. The Word of God is a wonderful bastion against such temptations. In this wicked world there is no way we can completely avoid Satan's attempts to bring these temptations to us. However there is one great protection and that is the Word of God. Immediately your mind is confronted with an evil thought, begin to quote Scripture, especially the precious promises of God, and continue to quote Scripture until the evil thoughts have been driven out of your mind and the beautiful truths in the messages of God take possession of the mind.

> Whereby are given unto us exceeding great and precious promises: that by these ye might be partakers of the divine nature, having escaped the corruption that is in the world through lust.   2 Peter 1:4

> Let this mind be in you, which was also in Christ Jesus.   Philippians 2:5

There is power in quoting Scripture, for the Psalmist says,

Thy word have I hid in mine heart, that I might not sin against thee.

Psalm 119:11

Sadly, there are many, even amongst Christian ministers, who fail to warn
against   pernicious practice of masturbation. However we must follow
          tements of Scripture. We realize that young people struggle
          any challenges and face perplexing problems. Young people
          aster now than they did one hundred years ago, which means
          escence and adolescence at a younger age. Generally speak-
          xity of life would advise young people today to marry later
          stom one hundred years ago. Therefore you are facing a
          d between coming to the physical maturity of adolescence
a   s for married life. This unquestionably puts great pres-
su   le, especially because of the media's debasing influence
up   society.
          n the nineteenth century concepts that masturbation can
seric   ntal health and emotional stability. Yet new evidence
is ma   vho are not strongly of a Christian persuasion to have
a seco   neful effects of masturbation. From our perspectives
as edu   and physician we sense one very serious problem. Every mental health problem which does not have a physical cause can be traced to
self centeredness. Nothing is more likely to cause a mental breakdown,
despondency or depression than self centeredness. Solitary acts directed
towards self-gratification will affect your mental health and your emotional
stability.

Masturbation undertaken by young people affects their emotions, feeling of self worth and their security in life. There are other evidences based
upon physiological effects which indicate, especially for males, that the loss
of seminal fluid leads to the loss of the trace mineral zinc which is highly
concentrated in the testes of the male. This is also crucial for the function
of the brain and some physicians now recognize that promiscuous practices
of any kind, not only masturbation, do affect the function of the brain. There
is a grave concern that this "harmless exploration" as some refer to masturbation, does indeed have serious emotional consequences. Dr. David
Horrobin, of Oxford University, relates problems which can result from zinc
deficiency. He states,

> Zinc deficiency has particularly profound effects on the male, because extraor-
> dinary amounts of zinc are found in the testicles and in the prostate gland. The
> amount of zinc in semen is such that one ejaculation may get rid of all the zinc
> that can be absorbed from the intestines in one day.
>
> In humans, among the most consistent effect of zinc deficiency are changes
> in mood and behavior. There is depression, extreme irritability, apathy and even

in some circumstances, behavior which looks like schizophrenia. . . . It is even possible, given the importance of zinc for the brain, that nineteenth century moralists were correct when they said that repeated masturbation could make one mad!   –David Harrobin, M.D., PhD, 1981, *Zinc*, Vitabooks, Inc., 8

Another highly qualified physician, this time from Harvard University, agrees.

We hate to say it but in a zinc-deficient adolescent, sexual excitement and excessive masturbation might precipitate insanity.   –Carl Pfeiffer, PhD, MD, *Zinc and Other Micronutrients,* 1978, Keats Publishing, Inc., 35

Mature adults must exert every effort to help children and youth understand these issues and to provide them with counsel which will help them to have victory over the temptation. One must start with the daily surrender of the life to Jesus, asking for Christ to take control of that life and preserve one from expressing or indulging these weaknesses. There are other issues. Eat regularly food which is plain and healthful, and not in too large quantities. Exercise vigorously, especially in useful work which is also a bastion against temptation. Guard carefully what is heard and seen. We also need to avoid the influence of those whose lives are impure. As soon as an evil thought comes to mind, ask God to take it away. As we have said earlier, focus upon quoting Scripture until the immoral thought has been eradicated from your mind.

   If you find yourselves in situations which stimulate your thinking in the wrong direction, ask the Lord for strength to move immediately away from that situation. Under no circumstances can we tolerate sin or sinful thoughts. The regular daily study of the Bible provides our minds with the spiritual food necessary to be able to quote Scripture when we are tempted by Satan. The Word of God, studied and memorized, would give great strength to overcome all temptations. Some have said that nothing in the Bible talks directly against masturbation. Some have found one or two texts that might imply biblical pronouncement, but certainly the Bible does address the issue in the general sense. We repeat again the statement of Jesus in His sermon on the Mount in which He says,

But I say unto you, That whosoever looketh on a woman to lust after her hath committed adultery with her already in his heart.   Matthew 5:28

Masturbation is usually associated with fantasy thoughts of sexual relationships with someone of the opposite sex. This is clearly condemned by Christ. Always thank God that He does not leave you without help in the battle over this temptation. Remember, Jesus had to battle all sins, yet He never yielded to temptation. There is no doubt that fierce temptations were placed before Him by the arch-deceiver. Yet in all things Jesus was victorious, therefore He is able to provide victory.

> Now unto him that is able to keep you from falling, and to present you faultless before the presence of his glory with exceeding joy. Jude 24

God has provided abundant grace to overcome the tempter.

> Forasmuch then as Christ hath suffered for us in the flesh, arm yourselves likewise with the same mind: for he that hath suffered in the flesh hath ceased from sin; That he no longer should live the rest of his time in the flesh to the lusts of men, but to the will of God. 1 Peter 4:1, 2

Christ's strength is always available in our fight against every temptation when we are submitted to His grace and power.

13

Does Dress Really Matter?

ON one occasion Colin was talking to a young lady who was bitterly complaining about the immoral intentions of some of the young men professing Christianity with whom she had dated. This young lady clearly had very strong and high moral standards. Certainly this was a praiseworthy position in this age of promiscuity and immorality. However it was not difficult to assess the situation. As Colin was talking to this young lady, he noted the provocative dress in which she was garbed—low neckline, sleeveless, high hem line—certainly sufficiently provocative to present the wrong signal to young men. Often young ladies are naïve. On the one hand they are desirous of attracting the attention of young men, even though immorality may be farthest from their thoughts. One sometimes wonders if it is the naïveté of some of these young women or are they simply living in denial?

In the possibility that some young lady readers do not understand fully the implications of dress, let us state plainly that from the male perspective, a young lady's character is judged by the way she dresses. Sadly, we face a generation in which many of the young people are far from conversion even though they may continue regular church attendance. Young men are making decisions. They are making evaluations, and much of that evaluation is made on the basis of dress. Converted, sincere young men are not looking for young women who are provocative in dress and behavior. They, themselves, are looking for mature, modest, ladylike young women from whom to choose a life partner. They do not desire a wife who demonstrates un-Christlike immodesty and, as a wife, would continue to exhibit sexually-provocative parts of her body before other men.

Colin turned to this young lady and asked her if she would mind looking in the mirror. Immediately Colin received a hostile response. She certainly was not naïve about the reason Colin had made this request. Thus she responded, "There is nothing wrong with the way I dress. It is just their dirty minds." The sharpness of her voice told another story. Deep down there was some understanding of that which Colin was implying. He went on to explain to her that there are Christian young men who do have high moral standards. They are under the control of Christ and are seeking purity in their lives. Colin further explained that such young men would not pay attention to any young lady who gave the appearance of being worldly and sensual in her life. They could not know that this young lady, in spite of her dress, had very high and settled moral convictions. Sometimes the children of darkness are wiser than the children of light.

> And the lord commended the unjust steward, because he had done wisely: for the children of this world are in their generation wiser than the children of light.
>
> Luke 16:8

In the business world—for example, the world of commerce—studies have been undertaken in an attempt to discover what is necessary to become a successful salesman or saleswoman or to make a positive impact as a leader. Of course many factors play into this situation. However one of those factors is dress. It has long ago been determined that evaluations are made in but a few seconds on the basis of dress, grooming and demeanor. Such decisions, rapid though they may be, are often decisive in areas such as door-to-door salesmanship, job interviews and credibility. Young people may say this is unfair and it may well be unfair in some respects. However, often the turn of mind, one's values and judgment, are reflected by the choice of dress.

Men and women of good training and wise judgment will know how to dress appropriately for circumstances. However, there are overriding principles in all these areas. Dress should be first and foremost, for the Christian, modest and attractive but not ostentatious. It should be healthy dress, appropriate to the climatic conditions that pertain. Dress should be clean. In the Christian context especially, dress should be wisely considered for the attendance of the house of the Lord. It says something concerning our lack of respect for the great God of the universe, and for our Savior, Jesus Christ, to enter the house of worship in casual and immodest clothing. Yet both are common in these days. Indeed, churches have been established which have encouraged casual dress as if it were a virtue rather than surely an insult to the King of kings and Lord of lords. Indeed, special dress wear should be put aside for the attendance at church services, special above what we normally would wear even if we are professionals in the work place.

However there are other issues that bespeak whether we are following in the pathway of the principles of heaven. True Christians do not dress in a manner to draw attention specifically to themselves. One seeking for a life companion should take very careful note of the dress of the members of the opposite sex. Those who adorn themselves with jewelry and makeup are not seeking to dress to the glory of God but rather to the glory of self. How magnificently the apostle Peter addressed this issue.

> Whose adorning let it not be that outward adorning of plaiting the hair, and of wearing of gold, or of putting on of apparel, but let it be the hidden man of the heart, in that which is not corruptible, even the ornament of a meek and quiet spirit, which is in the sight of God of great price.   1 Peter 3:3, 4

You will notice that Peter was placing the emphasis not upon the outward adorning, which is the way of the world and of those who are seeking only to draw attention to themselves, but the real adorning of a Christian, which is the ornament of a holy and consecrated spirit. So that, rather than drawing attention to ourselves, we are drawing attention to the Savior who is seeking to gather to Himself the faithful, humble, dedicated in the world.

The Old Testament also testifies to the problem of worldly ornamentation.

> Moreover the Lord saith, Because the daughters of Zion are haughty, and walk with stretched forth necks and wanton eyes, walking and mincing as they go, and making a tinkling with their feet: Therefore the Lord will smite with a scab the crown of the head of the daughters of Zion, and the Lord will discover their secret parts. In that day the Lord will take away the bravery of their tinkling ornaments about their feet, and their cauls, and their round tires like the moon, The chains, and the bracelets, and the mufflers, The bonnets, and the ornaments of the legs, and the headbands, and the tablets, and the earrings, The rings, and nose jewels, The changeable suits of apparel, and the mantles, and the wimples, and the crisping pins, The glasses, and the fine linen, and the hoods, and the veils. And it shall come to pass, that instead of sweet smell there shall be stink; and instead of a girdle a rent; and instead of well set hair baldness; and instead of a stomacher a girding of sackcloth; and burning instead of beauty.   Isaiah 3:16–24

Paul also adds his testimony so that we are not left in doubt that mode of dress is an important issue.

> In like manner also, that women adorn themselves in modest apparel, with shamefacedness and sobriety; not with broided hair, or gold, or pearls, or costly array; But (which becometh women professing godliness) with good works.   1 Timothy 2:9, 10

We believe that the principles of these counsels apply to young men as well as to young women. We have seen young men dressed only in a tank top and shorts entering the sacred, dedicated sanctuary of the Lord. This should be sufficient warning to any young lady that such a man has no understanding of the reverence and the greatness of God and is not a man yet ready to become a marriage partner.

Now we hasten to say that there may be those who will come to church wholly inappropriately dressed. Nevertheless, they themselves, as they learn more of the greatness of God, the majesty of His person and the matchless love which He has shed upon us, in return out of love and reverence for Him, will understand how to dress in God's sanctuary. Colin remembers studying the gospel with a lady and her husband. When they first came to the church, the wife was made up with heavy cosmetics and large amounts of jewelry. However, she noticed the modesty and the simplicity of the dress of the other women in the church. On one afternoon, in the middle of a Bible study, she suddenly asked, "What are the church's rules on dress?" Colin pointed out that it was not so much the rules of the church but it was the counsel of God given through Paul and Peter which defined the manner in which ladies should dress in the church. Then he concluded by saying, "What God is looking for is not efforts to draw the attention of men and women to us but rather that each one of us may draw people to Jesus our Savior." The response of this dear lady was simply, "That is beautiful." When she attended church the next week, so transformed was her appearance, that it took some members a little time to recognize her as the woman who had been attending the church for some months. Not only did this reflect a change of dress, it reflected the conversion of this woman, who was transformed from a woman who, in the community, was known as a troublemaker, to a woman who became known as one of the most loving Christians in that community. She visited every home to apologize for her previous conduct.

We return to young people. In your youth find the most appropriate attire you can so that you will honor God at all times and so that your service will be well pleasing unto the Lord. Such young people will attract other young people of Christian quality and virtue and will be much more likely to find a life spouse who shares their God-given values.

Let it be remembered that dowdy or unkempt clothing do not bespeak our love for Christ. We must ever be neat and tidy in our apparel and thus represent our Lord, and our respect and love for Him.

14

Unequally Yoked Together
with Unbelievers

PAUL in His teachings commanded,

> Be ye not unequally yoked together with unbelievers: for what fellowship hath
> righteousness with unrighteousness? and what communion hath light with dark-
> ness.   2 Corinthians 6:14

This is a command, which cannot be put aside without very serious consequences. Satan's effort is to deceive godly young people and to confuse their
minds so that they make irrational decisions which impact upon the rest of
their lives. Youth and young people must seek guidance from the Lord and
godly counselors so that they employ clear-minded thinking in the choice
of a life partner.

The Bible is replete with the consequences of choosing unwise spouses
who do not share the same dedication, who do not believe the same tran-
scendent truths of the Word of God, or spouses who are willing to compromise at the first hint of opposition or ridicule. Obviously such vacillat-
ing young people have not established the truth in their hearts and in their
lives and certainly not in their homes.

For many generations in the past, the above text was commonly used in
counseling and admonishing young people who were reaching maturity and
when they were considering seeking a marriage companion. Many church
denominations refused to provide pastors to perform weddings unless the
couple were united together in the same church fellowship. Many church
buildings were reserved for weddings of those only who were of the faith
of that church. Such a stance by today's standards seems cruel and lacking
in understanding. However with such strict guidelines it was far more difficult for young people to ignore the serious consequences which results
from such an unwise union. It attested to the fact that the pathway of
"mixed" marriages is fraught with many dangers. These dangers included
conflict between the parents over which church was God's church and as
to which church their children would attend. The conflict between the dif-

ferent beliefs of the parents sometimes had striking impact in that it so often caused confusion in the minds of the children and led them to reject all religion, which they perceived to be divisive, and in consequence led to argumentation and strife.

Some have interpreted the idea of being "unequally yoked together with unbelievers" too narrowly. They have applied it only to those who are not professing Christians, those who follow non-Christian religions or those who are avowed atheists or agnostics. Of course these are unbelievers. However, the criteria of an unbeliever must be looked at more closely than in the past. Even fifty years ago many recognized that this text applied to Roman Catholics marrying Protestants or Protestants marrying Roman Catholics. That was certainly a valid interpretation, because these faiths had many vastly different beliefs. Protestantism was built upon *sola Scriptura*, its faith was built upon the basis of the Bible alone. Roman Catholicism is built upon the Bible *and* church tradition. The Roman Catholic Church sanctions many practices which Protestants of that age traced back to the pagan religions of Babylon, Assyria, Egypt, Greece and Rome.

The Roman Catholic Church had a practice of refusing to perform, what they call, a "nuptial mass" unless the non-Catholic partner signed a binding agreement that the children would be brought up by the Roman Catholic spouse-to-be in the Roman Catholic faith. Obviously this was of deep concern to Protestants, who urged Protestant young people not to forge such a union. Certainly this was rightly judged as being "unequally yoked together with unbelievers," even though both partners were professing Christians.

The concerns went deeper. Most Protestants were opposed to their children marrying a spouse of a different faith. For example the Evangelicals and Presbyterians generally taught the doctrine of predestination whereby it is believed that God preordains men and women either to eternal salvation or eternal burning torment. However, others, such as Methodists and Free Will Baptists, taught that salvation is offered to all: God does not manipulate, God does not coerce, and therefore He permits humans to accept, reject or neglect His great salvation. These doctrinal differences were considered to be of such magnitude that it was seen to be unwise for a young man from one church to marry a young woman from the other church.

However, today, we believe that "being unequally yoked together with unbelievers" goes much further. Almost every church of Christendom is divided today. Some sincerely establish their faith upon the foundational doctrines and practices which were established at the origin of that church, while many others have deviated far from those original beliefs, practices and principles, believing that there can be a valid faith which allows for a more liberal interpretation of Scripture. Young people professing quite different faiths may attend the same church, and hold membership in that church. It is essential for young people to establish their beliefs, their doctrinal foundations and their practice of the Christian faith in such a way that they know the kind of home which they desire to establish.

Dedicated young people need to be careful not to marry those who do not have a deep love for God and for His church and who have only nominal adherence to their faith. What a heartache it is for the one who is dedicated to the Lord, and who constantly studies God's Word and craves the fellowship of his/her spouse in Bible study and in Christian dialogue so that they might learn together the will of God in their lives. When the other spouse has no interest, neglects family worship, has no desire to seek to understand the responsibilities either as a spouse or as a parent, and does not engage in daily spiritual life nor seek the wisdom of God in decision making or the rearing of the children in godly habits of life, the union is unequal. We sincerely believe that simply because two people are members of the same denomination does not in itself fulfill the requirement to be "not unequally yoked together with unbelievers." We have seen the tragedy of our friends of boyhood and youth being unequally yoked together with unbelievers. Below we recount a couple of cases.

We grew up in the city of Newcastle in Australia. We were privileged to have a godly home where both our parents were united in spiritual beliefs, goals and practices. This had a great stabilizing effect upon our lives. It was clear to us that our parents loved God above everything else. Therefore there was no ambivalence in our lives, no uncertainty, no conflict in these areas of spiritual life. Surely this had the most profound impact upon our own decision to follow Christ and to be led by Him into His service.

However, some of our friends did not have the same upbringing. One man with whom we were friends attended the same church, heard the same sermons and participated in the other meetings of the church. As a teenager he showed considerable and earnest interest in the spiritual life of the church and even more interest in spiritual issues. The three of us attended the same university together. We spent considerable time together. During this time he followed his religious practices. Where he went wrong was in his choice of a life partner. Instead of marrying a woman of his own faith he married a woman of a very different faith, though a professing—but not really a practicing—Christian. It did not take long after marriage for him to become irregular in his church attendance and, no doubt, lacking the support of a strongly Christian wife, his own personal Christian life began to fall apart, until eventually, though he was very successful in his profession, he lost his way and even to this day he is still far from the Lord, to our great anguish.

Years after his marriage Colin had the opportunity to talk with this friend of youth. They walked and talked together as Colin sought to urge him to reconsider the direction of his life. After a long dialogue, he uttered the tragic words to Colin, "Col, it is too late. I chose the wrong wife." All Colin's urging for him to take a stand for God and for His saving grace seemed to fall on unresponsive ears. Colin urged him to take such a stand for the sake of his children whom he now had fathered and also for the influence that it might be upon his wife. But it seemed that no longer was he open to such counsel.

The second case was another young man, indeed, the closest friend whom we had when we were training to be teachers in a Christian college. The three of us had attended the same church and the same Christian high school. This friend's father was a minister of the gospel and his mother a godly woman. He had made stands at altar calls at college. There is no question that the Holy Spirit was moving on his heart. But during his college life, his eyes became infatuated with one of the prettiest girls on campus. There is no doubt that she was an attractive young lady. She was of the same faith, indeed, her parents had been missionaries in the South Pacific Islands. But for whatever reason, her commitment to the Lord did not have the same beauty as her physical attractiveness. No doubt infatuated by the personal charm of this young lady, our friend was somehow able to put aside the other characteristics and her obvious lack of spiritual depth or interest. It was plain even at college that she had but a superficial interest in religion. The evidence, though, was not that of a deep and dedicated commitment to her Lord. They professed the same religion. This wife proved to be a stronger personality than our friend. She influenced him greatly, as did other skeptical folk who had become his close acquaintances. By fatal steps his faith weakened. Commitment to the Lord wavered and though also successful in his chosen profession, he lost his faith altogether and became agnostic.

Years later, Colin was walking with this friend, now totally devoid of Christ in his life. They walked along a waterway. Just prior to this stroll his minister father had talked with Colin and he had pled with Colin to do all he could to lead his son back to his Savior. Of course that was Colin's desire. Thus Colin dialogued earnestly about his need of Christ and the reestablishing of his connection with his Lord. Once again, all was to no avail. He made the tragic statement to Colin, "I know that you are much happier than I am. I can see that you are very fulfilled in your life. However this is the life that I have chosen and I have to live with it." The reader can understand the sorrow which Colin experienced. It is so difficult and painful to realize that a friend who at one time espoused many of the same concepts as oneself, has lost his trust and faith in the Lord.

The anguish of Colin's heart was deepened when his father later came back to talk with him, for he had learned that they had met and talked together. His plea to Colin was, "Did ——— give you any hope that one day he might return to the Lord?" What could Colin say to this anguished father which would be truthful? Colin searched for words but all he could say was, "——— is not yet ready to make a commitment to the Lord." In the three-and-one-half decades which have transpired since that dialogue, the pastor has gone to his rest and our friend is still, to our human evaluation, outside of the saving power of his Savior.

We can only uphold before you the perfect principles of heaven. The counsel which is given can be put aside only at the risk of eternal consequences. Christian young people, make your own dedication to the Lord, and refrain from marrying anyone who does not share the same faith and your deep dedication to Jesus and His saving grace.

15

Bible Principles Which, if Ignored, Contribute to Divorce

FROM the study of God's Word we can discover principles which, if ignored or disobeyed, greatly contribute to the likelihood of divorce. Not all these passages deal directly with divorce. However, they are principles of life which, if not heeded, will lead to great stress within the marriage and often bring division between married couples, and which can greatly diminish the life of the marriage.

1. *Responsibility* is now uncommon before a marriage. However the Christian will not marry until he has developed a high level of responsibility. This will affect many issues in a marriage. Irresponsibility with money can create debt and can greatly diminish the stability of the lifestyle of the marriage. If one spouse is irresponsible, great grief may be brought to the other spouse and bitter, contested problems may result. Irresponsibility can also lead to poor parenting and poor habits of household tidiness. It can lead to waste of time, and to being occupied with things which are of little importance, to the neglect of those things which are important. The Bible addresses this issue. It refers to the irresponsible as unstable. For example, Jacob's older son Reuben was described as

Unstable as water, thou shalt not excel;   Genesis 49:4

Obviously, Reuben lacked great moral integrity and was weak in the leadership which rightly should have been his as the eldest son of the family.

James describes an unstable man in these words,

A double-minded man is unstable in all his ways.   James 1:8

In this case the instability comes from double-mindedness. If one is double-minded his mind will change frequently, and his actions will lead him to treat his wife kindly when in "the right mood," but then, when his mood changes, he may treat her cruelly. The same can happen in his treatment of his children. Often the irresponsible spouse will be easily drawn into an adulterous relationship.

Having eyes full of adultery, and that cannot cease from sin; beguiling unstable souls: a heart they have exercised with covetous practices; cursed children.

2 Peter 2:14

A man who leads a double life does not have victory over the carnal desires of his heart and, with such a mind, he causes anguish to other people and seeks to use subtlety to win the affection of someone other than his wife. This is a tragedy, not only for his wife but also for his children. Every effort should be made when considering marriage to be certain that the suitor has godly responsibility and that he can see the same quality in the one to whom he is considering pledging his life.

2. *Morality*.

> Oh that I had in the wilderness a lodging place of wayfaring men; that I might leave my people, and go from them! for they be all adulterers, an assembly of treacherous men. And they bend their tongues like their bow for lies: but they are not valiant for the truth upon the earth; for they proceed from evil to evil, and they know not me, saith the Lord.   Jeremiah 9:2–3

Here Jeremiah declares the generation of his day to be adulterers. It is important to note the characteristics which are associated with the adulterers. Firstly they are called treacherous men, then they are called liars. It is a normal consequence for adulterers to lie about their adultery, to attempt to cover up the wickedness of their lives. Therefore they cannot speak the truth. It is not possible for a spouse who engages in adulterous activities to be a trustworthy spouse or parent.

King Solomon had very important words to say about the adulterer. There probably has not been a worse womanizer than Solomon, so no doubt he was speaking from the tragedies of his own life and experience.

> To keep from the evil woman, from the flattery of the tongue of a strange woman. Lust not after her beauty in thine heart; neither let her take thee with her eyelids. For by means of a whorish woman a man is brought to a piece of bread; and the adulteress will hunt for the precious life. Can a man take fire in his bosom, and his clothes not be burned? Can one go upon hot coals, and his feet not be burned? So he that goeth in to his neighbour's wife; whosoever toucheth her shall not be innocent.   Proverbs 6:24–29

All too frequently a husband or a wife is seduced or seduces someone outside the marriage bond. Only consider the sacredness of the marriage vow and the consequences of its violation. There are few words which can describe the enormity of the consequences of such a violation of God's principles. Men especially have a penchant for the desire to claim many conquests from the favors of the opposite sex. Increasingly today women fall for this perverse lifestyle. Today there are some spouses who make agreement together to sleep around with other people. In some places clubs have been set up for couples to experience the "excitement" of sleeping with another individual. How perverse! how disgusting! are such practices.

When we were students at the University of Sydney, we met a man who was a self-confessed libertarian. He said he had a wonderful arrangement with his wife in which she could sleep with other men and he could sleep with other women. He saw this as great liberation and freedom. However, some time later he came to us in great distress, for his wife had left him for another man with whom she had slept. Once again the wisdom of Solomon must be considered.

> There is a way which seemeth right unto a man, but the end thereof are the ways of death. Even in laughter the heart is sorrowful; and the end of that mirth is heaviness. The backslider in heart shall be filled with his own ways: and a good man shall be satisfied from himself.   Proverbs 14:12–14

The wicked man, the one who practices adultery, brings great grief upon himself as well as to his spouse. Colin recalls, after preaching a sermon, a woman obviously in great distress and under conviction by the sermon, who told Colin she must talk with him. This Colin did while away from other people's ears, nevertheless in the open courtyard of the church. However before she could express herself, she burst into uncontrollable sobbing. Eventually, gaining some composure, she stated she had a good husband and two lovely children, but she was having an affair with another man and she could not forgive herself. While the Scripture says "The wages of sin is death," we also often have to pay bitter consequences now for our sin. No wonder Solomon said,

> The way of transgressors is hard.   Proverbs 13:15

It is sin which robs us of our peace of mind, of our calm joy and satisfaction. So destructive of the marriage bond is adultery, that it is the only ground for which God authorizes divorce and remarriage.

> And I say unto you, Whosoever shall put away his wife, except it be for fornication, and shall marry another, committeth adultery: and whoso marrieth her which is put away doth commit adultery.   Matthew 19:9

3. *Sexual perversions.* We have known numbers of marriages which have been dissolved because of the homosexuality of the husband or the lesbian activities of the wife. Even though children have been born to the marriage there is no guarantee that a spouse is not engaged in homosexual or lesbian behavior. Colin once had a secretary whose marriage floundered on the discovery that her husband was a practicing homosexual. We have known pastors and even an evangelist whose marriages collapsed because of their practice of homosexuality. We know of yet another case where a minister put away his wife because of her lesbianism. In most of these cases children were born to the marriage. It seems as if some believe that if they marry, their orientation will change. However, the only hope for true and permanent change is the power of the all-conquering Savior. Rare though it is, we have known men who, grasping upon the help of Divine power, have forged successful marriages. It is more difficult today when the perversity of such unnatural tendency is approved by major segments of society and many well-known churches.

As homosexuals and lesbians flaunt their unholy practices, they are described not as abominations unto the Lord, but simply as "alternative lifestyles." We hasten to add that the lifestyle of the fornicator or adulterer is just as surely an abomination unto the Lord. Scripture is plain on these issues. Referring back to the shocking abominations just prior to the Noachian flood and to the days just before the destruction of Sodom and Gomorrah, the Bible leaves no doubt as to the perverseness of these activities.

> But before they lay down, the men of the city, even the men of Sodom, compassed the house round, both old and young, all the people from every quarter: And they called unto Lot, and said unto him, Where are the men which came in to thee this night? bring them out unto us, that we may know them.
>
> Genesis 19:4–5

> Even as Sodom and Gomorrha, and the cities about them in like manner, giving themselves over to fornication, and going after strange flesh, are set forth for an example, suffering the vengence of eternal fire.   Jude 7

> And turning the cities of Sodom and Gomorrha into ashes condemned them with an overthrow, making them an ensample unto those that after should live ungodly.   2 Peter 2:6

> Likewise also as it was in the days of Lot; they did eat, they drank, they bought, they sold, they planted, they builded; But the same day that Lot went out of Sodom it rained fire and brimstone from heaven, and destroyed them all. Even thus shall it be in the day when the Son of man is revealed.   Luke 17:28–30

So filled with homosexuality was Sodom that its name became a synonym for homosexuality with the designation "sodomy."

God condemns lesbian practices.

> Wherefore God also gave them up to uncleanness, through the lusts of their own hearts, to dishonour their own bodies between themselves: . . . For this cause God gave them up unto vile affections: for even their women did change the natural use into that which is against nature.   Romans 1:24, 26

Just as surely God condemns homosexual practices.

> Thou shalt not lie with mankind, as with womankind: it is abomination.
>
> Leviticus 18:22

> And likewise also the men, leaving the natural use of the woman, burned in their lust one toward another; men with men working that which is unseemly, and receiving in themselves that recompence of their error which was meet.
>
> Romans 1:27

> Know ye not that the unrighteous shall not inherit the kingdom of God? Be not
> deceived: neither fornicators, nor idolaters, nor adulterers, nor effeminate, nor
> abusers of themselves with mankind.   1 Corinthians 6:9

That such practices are condoned in professed Christian nations pinpoints
the degradation of the age in which we live. There are other practices which
also have led to the dissolution of marriage such as bestiality, the vile practice of sexual relationship with animals. God leaves us in no doubt about
the perverseness of such acts.

> Neither shalt thou lie with any beast to defile thyself therewith: neither shall
> any woman stand before a beast to lie down thereto: it is confusion.
>   Leviticus 18:23

In some ways, even more shocking in its consequences is the increasing
frequency of incest when a parent takes advantage of his or her own child
to perform sexual acts with them. The psychological damage to the child
may never be fully removed. How essential is the gospel of Jesus to control the evil imaginations of the carnal heart of men and women. A spouse
has no alternative but to separate the children so abused from the offending parent. To fail to do so may later bring the wrath of the child upon the
parent who failed to protect the child from such wicked abuse.

4. *The use of alcohol.* Myriads of marriages have been destroyed when one
or both of the spouses fall victim to alcohol. The wise man said,

> He that loveth pleasure shall be a poor man: he that loveth wine and oil shall
> not be rich.   Proverbs 21:17

However, Solomon much more strongly details the tragedy of alcoholic
drink in the life of human beings.

> Look not thou upon the wine when it is red, when it giveth his colour in the
> cup, when it moveth itself aright. At the last it biteth like a serpent, and stingeth
> like an adder. Thine eyes shall behold strange women, and thine heart shall ut-
> ter perverse things. Yea, thou shalt be as he that lieth down in the midst of the
> sea, or as he that lieth upon the top of a mast.   Proverbs 23:31–34

The strong words of verse 32 liken the danger of alcohol to the bite of a
serpent or the sting of an adder. What a warning this is, for, indeed, there
are few drugs more likely to lead to diabolical consequences in the home
than imbibing of alcoholic drinks. However, in verse 33 Solomon addresses
a very important aspect of that which will destroy a marriage. Alcohol
greatly affects the function of the brain. It very rapidly anesthetizes the
conscience, making it well-nigh impossible to make wise and moral decisions. One of its first deadly effects is upon the frontal lobe of the brain—
the cerebrum. This is where the decisions, choices, and moral values are

made. When the brain is affected by alcohol almost inevitably the conscience fails to warn of the wrong which is taking place.

Alcohol changes the moods and the emotions of an individual. Such a
one, who under normal circumstances, might be wise, with a calm disposition, now becomes belligerent, dangerous and even violent. These characteristics can bring tremendous stress upon a marriage and may be the prime
cause of divorce. It is the cerebrum where our minds can restrain the carnal cravings of the body. Without such restraint, the Holy Spirit cannot minister to our minds, and thus actions take place which we would never dream
of undertaking otherwise.

Those who advocate moderate drinking forget the fact that neurons are
destroyed by alcohol and that no matter how little alcohol is consumed, it
brings a diminishing of our ability to hear the voice of God and to retain
moral integrity deeply essential to our own salvation. Alcohol weakens our
ability to be a wise and faithful spouse and parent.

Every year millions of divorces take place either directly or indirectly
as a result of the imbibing of alcohol.

16

Real Life Experiences with Alcohol

IN 1974 Russell attended the tenth anniversary of his graduation from the University of Sydney as a physician. To his shock, three of the young former medical students with whom he had studied were dead. All three had committed suicide. They had become alcoholics, and became so depressed with their lives that after all the enormous effort they had put forth to obtain their medical qualifications, they thought that life was not worth living.

So difficult had been the course that of the six hundred who commenced it, only two hundred and forty ever graduated and of those two hundred and forty, only ninety of them graduated in the six years it took to study medicine in those days. The others had all needed to repeat at least one year of their course. One of the graduates had to repeat every year of his course, but did graduate after twelve years of study.

Yet despite all this effort, they took their own lives, destroying the happiness of their wives and children. Alcohol is the greatest drug curse in the world. If alcohol had first been discovered in the twenty-first century, it would have been thoroughly investigated with rigorous testing. It would have been found to destroy the brain, the liver, the heart, the stomach, the nerves, the pancreas. It would have been found to cause more crimes of violence, murders and acts of immorality than heroin, cocaine, marijuana, amphetamines and all other drugs combined. Research would have demonstrated that it was the source of more marriage break-ups and disharmony than all other causes. As a result it would have been declared to be an illegal drug in every civilized country of the world. In some Asian nations purveyors of alcohol would have been hanged.

Yet because alcohol has been used from ancient times and because it provides an enormous source of tax revenue for many nations, it is openly promoted in all forms of advertising media. Sporting heroes think it manly to get drunk after a match. Especially in Western countries, this has led to charges of rape by married sportsmen. Others have been found guilty of inflicting bodily harm and even murder under the influence of alcohol.

Those young doctors from Russell's graduating class who committed suicide left behind widows and children. In this way alcohol had savagely destroyed the happiness and welfare of the family. One of these doctors had been a practicing Christian as a medical student. He belonged to a Protestant denomination which during the eighteenth to nineteenth centuries had promoted abstinence from the imbibing of alcohol in every form. But as the twentieth century progressed there was a relaxation of this wise standard. Perhaps if that standard had been maintained this fine young medical student would have eschewed alcohol and his marriage and family would have been preserved and not fractured by his self-destruction.

Marriages can be destroyed by alcohol at later stages. Russell recollects an incident, which occurred in his student days, which illustrates this fact. The Professor of Psychiatry was leading a group of students, of whom Russell was one, through the wards of a Psychiatric Hospital, in order to tutor them on aspects of certain psychiatric illnesses. The students were preparing to enter one ward, when the professor sternly forbade them. They were surprised for they had not been informed of any such prohibition. Querying the professor in order to ascertain the reasons for his command, he informed the group that every patient in that ward was a physician whose mind had been destroyed by alcohol. The professor discerned it inappropriate for medical students to see physicians in such a state.

Russell has often wondered over the years whether the professor's restraining order was wise. Since records show that physicians suffer from alcoholism twice as frequently as the average incidence in the Australian population, perhaps the viewing of the pitiful situation of these doctors may have served as a sober warning to the doctors in training. Those men through their mental deterioration and long-term hospitalization had rent their marriages.

Russell remembers in 1967 relieving a physician on vacation. As he read the management of the physician's patients, Russell was very concerned. He was irrational in his prescribing of medication, seriously unprofessional in his physical examinations, especially of younger women, and careless. Russell noted bottles of alcohol in various cupboards in his clinic. Upon his return this doctor, who was divorced, admitted that his breath always stank of alcohol, but added, "But my patients love me just the same." And indeed they did. Many regarded the weekly injections he was giving them as keeping them alive, when they were totally unnecessary.

Men and women, in all walks of life, not infrequently endanger the lives of those who use them as experts in their field, when, in fact, their skills and judgment have been seriously impaired by alcohol. Many soon lose their ability to be the breadwinner in the family, causing serious family disharmony and unhappiness.

We experienced the misery of alcohol in our own family. Our loving parents were teetotalers. But our maternal grandfather, though not an alcoholic, was nevertheless a relatively heavy beer drinker. He fathered five sons and six daughters, of whom our mother was the youngest child in the family, born when her father was forty-seven and her mother forty-two.

When he had imbibed alcohol, our grandfather's Irish temper was very short indeed, as his sons learned when they received heavy beatings, even for relatively minor infractions. Our grandmother was a loving Christian woman who lived up to her marriage vow "to love and honor" her husband "for better or for worse." And worse it was much of the time.

The youngest son, our Uncle Frederick, who was the ninth child in the family, spent most of his time staying with his married sisters and a bachelor older brother, in order to escape the ire of our grandfather. Our Uncle Thomas did the mail deliveries in a small town called Kurri Kurri about twenty-five miles from the family home. Fred, at sixteen years of age, had completed his education. On one occasion he was staying with our Uncle Thomas, who was twelve years senior to Fred.

One day Tom returned home to discover that Fred was not there, as he normally was. Tom searched the small coal-mining town to no avail. He visited the small hospital and visited the police station without learning information of Fred's whereabouts. The year was 1926. Believing that Fred must have returned to the family home, Tom took the train the next morning in order to confirm his suspicions. The family possessed no telephone in that era.

For the first time our grandparents were alerted to Fred's disappearance. Our loving grandmother immediately visited the police. They showed little concern once they discovered the antipathy between Fred and his Dad, suggesting that he had probably returned after a few days, or perhaps he had joined the crew on a ship, and they would later receive a letter from some exotic overseas port. The police did examine Tom's home and found no evidence of foul play.

As days became weeks and weeks months, Fred's file in the police missing persons folders was eventually removed out of sight and out of mind. However our grandmother continued to expect that letter posted in a far away port. She daily peered outside the front fence, lest Fred had returned, but had hesitated to come inside, fearing severe corporal punishment from his father for his disappearance. There was a street light outside the home. Night after night our grandmother strained her eyes through her bedroom window, eagerly seeking her beloved son. Her prayers never ceased on his behalf. Her grief and agonizing uncertainty knew no bounds.

About five years later, our grandmother perused a copy of *The Newcastle Morning Herald*. There she saw a photograph of a group of naval ratings from a warship docked in Sydney harbor. One was Fred! Grandmother wasted no time, in her joy, to take the slow, all-stop train the one-hundred-four miles south from Newcastle to Sydney. It took five hours. She made her way down through the ugly dock area to the wharf where the naval vessel was berthed.

Two naval ratings with rifles and fixed bayonets at the ready were guarding the gangplank, which led to the deck. Grandmother explained her mission to find her lost boy. One of the ratings, in compassion, volunteered to go to the captain and ask if he would see our grandmother. The captain consented and Grandmother was ushered into his command room.

After hearing an explanation of the problem, the captain searched for the name Frederick Bailey among his crew. No naval rating of that name was listed. Grandmother explained that it was most likely that he had changed his name. The captain agreed to cancel all day leave the following morning, to call a deck parade of every sailor, and to permit Grandmother to review the parade in order to identify her son.

True to his word, a full roll call was taken and Grandmother reviewed their faces, recognizing that between the age of sixteen and twenty-one some facial alteration was likely. But hope ended in despair. It was a case of mistaken identity. When the young man in the photograph was brought to meet our grandmother, he was not Fred. The five-hour return journey to Newcastle was the longest five-hour period in her life.

Fred was never found. Whether he disappeared and left off all contact with his family; whether he was abducted and murdered; or whether he fell down a disused coal mine and perished, or met with some other fate—we have no idea. But our grandmother never forgot her son.

On October 9, 1942 our grandmother was dying. She was delirious. We were just eighteen days short of our ninth birthday. Our oldest uncle, Oliver, accompanied our mother to the bedroom where Grandmother was dying so that she could say her last goodbyes. She died the following day. In her delirious state her mind was still focused on Fred. She imagined he was alive and still a little boy. Turning to our uncle and calling him by his Christian name initials she said, "J.O., don't forget to bath Fred." These were the last words our grandmother uttered. The pathos of those words still bring tears to our eyes as we write. What love of a mother for her lost boy—lost because he had to flee the family home to avoid the alcohol-induced anger of his father. What a curse that evil, dangerous drug is to family harmony.

There is joy, however, at the conclusion of this intrusion into family history. Our grandfather survived our grandmother by almost seven years. Our parents and we returned to live with him so that our mother could care for him. He had hated our grandmother's church-going. He told visitors from the church that they were unwelcome in his home. Yet despite all his disagreeable conduct, unbeknown to our grandmother, her loving, tender Christian life had been a witness to her spouse.

Five years after our grandmother's death at seventy-one years of age, without any prior indications of the least change of heart, Grandpa asked our mother to arrange for him to attend church. He was eighty-one now, but of an acute mind. Our mother almost fainted. He hated that church! But our grandfather was not one to argue with or query about this apparent change of heart.

We, immature at only thirteen years of age, both sat in church that day, our eyes fixed upon Grandpa. We said to one another, "It is not right that Grandpa is here, he's too wicked!" How we misunderstood the tender forgiveness of God and the power of the Holy Spirit. He was eventually baptized.

Grandfather lived another two years. What a transformation we witnessed! A grandfather whom we and all his other grandchildren had feared, became a loving, godly Grandpa. He even told our mother that he always knew he was married to a loving, godly wife. We hope he tells this to Grandmother on the resurrection day, for he never in the least indicated this fact while she was alive. We are sure he will! They lie buried together in Newcastle's Sandgate Cemetery. What a surprise our grandmother will receive on that glad day. Grandpa saved! Grandpa! He'll have a wonderful time telling her of his inner love for her, and the infinite love her witness led him to discover in his Savior.

If ever you become discouraged over an unbelieving spouse, please recall the story of our grandparents, John and Alice Bailey—God bless them! Is it possible that Grandmother claimed the following verses of Scripture,

If any brother hath a wife that believeth not, and she be pleased to dwell with him, let him not put her away. And the woman which hath an husband that believeth not, and if he be pleased to dwell with her, let her not leave him. For the unbelieving husband is sanctified by the wife, and the unbelieving wife is sanctified by the husband: else were your children unclean; but now are they holy. 1 Corinthians 7:12–14

17

Other Bible Principles Which, if Ignored, Contribute to Divorce

WHILE moral issues are major factors in many divorces, they are not the only issues. This chapter addresses some of the other factors.

5. *In-laws*. Often marriages are jeopardized by the breakdown of respect and communication with, or between, in-laws. We again remind the reader that you not only marry a spouse, you are joining a new family. This can add greatly to the complexity of marriage. If parents-in-law perceive that their child is being mistreated by their son- or daughter-in-law, great tension is created. Relationships between the two sets of in-laws may also be greatly strained. Every effort should be exerted by the young married couple to seek to respect their in-laws, and also to give them assurance that they are fully worthy of the responsibility which they share with the other spouse. It is equally essential that the parents-in-law seek to forge loving relationships with their child's spouse. So much is at stake! Not only is the harmony and support of the new marriage at stake, but the in-laws' access to any grandchildren is greatly affected. Few broken relationships are worse than those which occur within families. The unhappiness engendered can lead to lifelong misery and create bitter disputes between the spouses which can very easily lead to divorce. While we believe that parents-in-law must do all they can to help the young couple, the Bible also has clear warning to the young couple concerning their interpersonal relationships with their in-laws.

> For the son dishonoureth the father, the daughter riseth up against her mother, the daughter in law against her mother in law; a man's enemies are the men of his own house.   Micah 7:6

6. *Ill health.* All Christian married couples take sacred vows when they marry—vows of strict fidelity to one another—in sickness and in health, in prosperity and adversity. However, such difficult consequences in the future are often far from the thoughts of young men and women when they make those vows. Usually both contracting individuals are young, strong, apparently healthy and vigorous. It is not easy to envisage that one day as the years take their toll, the ravages of age will greatly change this situation. When the effects of aging of both spouses takes place in advanced years, usually there is little effect upon the marriage. However, when illness or accident permanently incapacitates one spouse at a relatively young age, the nuptial vows can quickly be forgotten. Will the other spouse still continue his or her love and attentive care as vowed at the marriage altar? Sadly, some spouses use the serious illness or incapacitation of their spouse to justify a divorce so that they can seek to marry someone else. But such is adultery. There are even occasions where the incapacitated spouse has suggested that he or she is no longer of any value to the healthy spouse and that he or she should seek another spouse. However, that is not a principle which comes from God. Sickness and grave injuries can be a great test to both the incapacitated spouse and the healthy spouse, but a true Christian will never violate his or her marriage pledge.

We make these comments while bearing deep compassion for those whose marriages are so despoiled by such unfortunate setbacks. However, the eternal rewards of heaven will far outweigh the burdens of this life. God will provide strength for every burden cheerfully endured in love for the incapacitated spouse, and love for Jesus. We recognize that these trials are ever so difficult when our spouse develops a mental illness. This undoubtedly is a severe test of marital fidelity. Only God can sustain the one living with a spouse so afflicted, or separated through hospitalization.

Regarding health, there are yet other issues to consider. If husbands and wives follow all Biblical principles of healthful living because they believe that their "body is the temple of the Holy Ghost" (1 Corinthians 6:19), they will "eat and drink to the glory of God" (1 Corinthians 10:31). This practice will greatly reduce the onset of early illness. When one spouse abuses the other spouse, causing anguish and grief, this abuse can precipitate physical as well as emotional disorders. So cruel is this abuse that if a spouse has mental or physical breakdown, the abusing partner may very well decide this to be an excuse for divorce declaring that the other spouse is no longer able to function effectively as a wife or husband. It is, however, essential that all seek to find God's health principles and achieve the best health, and pray for God's protection to keep each one from accident or injury. Health and strength is a great asset in the fulfillment of marriage responsibility both to the partner and also to the children who have been added to the family.

7. *Immaturity.* Immaturity takes many forms. Of course, it includes acting in ways which are the ways of those who are much younger. Immaturity is expressed in irresponsible behavior. Paul calls us to Christian stability in our understanding and practice.

> That we henceforth be no more children, tossed to and fro, and carried about with every wind of doctrine, by the sleight of men, and cunning craftiness, whereby they lie in wait to deceive; But speaking the truth in love, may grow up into him in all things, which is the head, even Christ.   Ephesians 4:14–15

Immature Christians often become immature spouses and immature parents. If young people are weak Christians, they lack the firm principles of God's Word to apply to their marriage responsibilities. Some misuse Christ's admonition to "become as little children" (Matthew 19:14; 18:3). This is not counsel for those contracting marriage to be simpletons, naïve or ignorant, but addresses conversion by which we live a life of implicit trust in God and His Word. Paul explains in which areas we are to be children and where we must be mature.

> Brethren, be not children in understanding: howbeit in malice be ye children, but in understanding be men.   1 Corinthians 14:20

This text certainly applies to the principles of a successful marriage. We need to have such love for each other that malice is not mature in our hearts one toward the other. However we must be mature in our understanding and wisdom of our responsibilities as husbands and wives and as parents. If one or both spouses are immature, ignorance of divine principles of life and adult responsibilities very quickly sours the marriage. Petty issues can quickly be inflamed into major disputes. Minor differences of opinion can raise tempers and even, at times, lead to physical abuse. Habits of interpersonal communication, when ineffective, all too commonly lead marriage partners to communicate uncivilly with each other. Dialogue has no place in conversation and reason is absent.

These habits soon affect communication with the children, and soon the children can hardly offer a civil word to each other or to their parents. Family love has fled out the backdoor of the home. The marriage becomes unhappy and leads to drudgery, and it becomes easy to contemplate separation or divorce. In every marriage, calm and careful conversation must be the foundation. Often, as a result of a frustrating argument, a spouse sulks over the disagreements and responds by walking away into prolonged silence and non-communication. All these are signs of immaturity and unfitness for marriage in the first place. Stress, frustration and bitterness all too often are the forerunners of the breakdown of the marriage. Development of mature Christian conduct is essential before marriage vows are taken.

8. *Jealousy,* especially unfounded jealousy, can make a powerful contribution to the wrecking of a marriage. It causes great grief to the suspicioned spouse. Often jealousy is built up on unfounded suspicion of the infidelity of the other marriage partner. We have known husbands who have dialogued with another woman, raising irrational suspicion of developing a romantic interest in the woman with whom they are dialoguing. Most commonly such jealousy is a result of insecurity and feelings of inadequacy by the other spouse. Insecure men also act in jealous passion against their wives, and such husbands may respond in sudden outbursts of anger, sometimes causing scenes in front of other men and women who may be within earshot of them. Such men are also prone to place terrible restrictions upon the movements and activities of their wives, so that life for the wives can become well nigh unbearable. No amount of assurances by the suspicioned one can allay the jealousy of such a one. That this kind of conduct takes place in the jealous spouse should not be surprising, for the wise man explained this well:

> For jealousy is the rage of a man: therefore he will not spare in the day of vengeance. Proverbs 6:34

> Set [wisdom] as a seal upon thine heart, as a seal upon thine arm: for love is strong as death; jealousy is cruel as the grave: the coals thereof are coals of fire, which hath a most vehement flame. Song of Solomon 8:6

Keep in mind that a jealous and suspicious suitor is almost certain to become a jealous and suspicious spouse.

How carefully should young people discern the jealous spirit of a suitor *before* marriage! That person should detect the overly close attention by a suitor which may wrongly be interpreted as devotion. Yet wise examination will discern the difference between loving attentions and jealous obsessions. To make a mistake in this issue can lead to lifelong hardships and misery.

We hasten to conclude that we are not addressing suspicions against an unfaithful spouse who might engender jealous emotions in his or her partner. There are those spouses who behave with members of the opposite sex in ways which are wholly inappropriate

9. *Finance*. Paul warns against the obsession that some have with money.

> For the love of money is the root of all evil: which while some coveted after, they have erred from the faith, and pierced themselves through with many sorrows. 1 Timothy 6:10

Beware of a spouse who is focused upon the accumulation of wealth, possessions and property. It is common for a woman or a man to desire to marry a wealthy spouse. It is just as common for the parents of a daughter to encourage her to marry a man who will have the resources to "care well for her." However, allowing this to become a primary goal bodes poorly for the marriage. One has only to understand the common occurrence of multiple marriages among the wealthy class to realize that money is not a guarantee of a happy marriage. On the other hand, we warn that a lazy man can just as quickly cause strain to a marriage. Often the wife has to become the primary breadwinner and provide for the family, and thus the family is left in active poverty resulting in tragic consequences.

There are other spouses who act irresponsibly with money. Isaiah identifies the financially irresponsible.

> Wherefore do ye spend money for that which is not bread? and your labour for that which satisfieth not?   Isaiah 55:2

Such a person wastes time and money on non-salvation issues and this may also lead to dire consequences creating crippling debt for the family. No Christian can honor God when he or she is irresponsible with the resources which God has entrusted to the family. Such a one robs the family of a reasonable life in this earth and jeopardizes the family's eternal destiny. What an example to the children! Once again, the marriage can flounder and lead to worse consequences.

If both spouses are financially irresponsible then there is constant grief. If only one is a careful financial manager, the other spouse should be wise enough to allow the responsible one to manage the household finances. All families should determine to be debt free. A budget should be established and carefully followed. It should provide not only for the necessities of the family but for the returning of a faithful tithe to the Lord and for sacrificial offerings to help those in need and the spread of the gospel.

10.   *The Hollywood myth.* Of course the Scriptures do not refer to Hollywood as such, but they do focus upon some of the negative consequences of the products which flood the cinemas, the television sets, the Internet, video and DVD stores. Hollywood represents all those media distributors— all who produce wickedness for the eyes and the ears of the human race. With rare exception, Hollywood specializes in violence and the flaunting of abominable sex practices. Its objective is to pander to the most debasing carnality of the human race. Its products not only rob audiences of the sober, sacred responsibilities of life, they fill minds with the most degrading thoughts imaginable to the human race. Those young people addicted to any forms of these productions are certainly unfit to accept the responsibility of marriage. No mind feasting upon media garbage can stay pure and balanced. The mind is polluted and diseased. It has no capacity to listen clearly to the Holy Spirit's promptings, any more than such a mind can contribute to the making of sound judgments and preparing one for marriage. Jesus presents wonderful promises to those who protect their minds from evil,

> Blessed are the pure in heart: for they shall see God.   Matthew 5:8

No one who feasts upon Hollywood can possess a pure mind. Paul clearly identifies that upon which the converted Christian's mind will dwell.

> Finally, brethren, whatsoever things are true, whatsoever things are honest, whatsoever things are just, whatsoever things are pure, whatsoever things are lovely, whatsoever things are of good report; if there be any virtue, and if there be any praise, think on these things.   Philippians 4:8

> But we all, with open face beholding as in a glass the glory of the Lord, are changed into the same image from glory to glory, even as by the Spirit of the Lord.   2 Corinthians 3:18

The Word of God says, "By beholding [Christ] we are changed." If we behold Christ we become changed into the image of God. To the contrary, if we behold Hollywood, we are changed into the image of Satan and therefore are wholly unfitted for heaven and therefore unfitted to even consider the role of a spouse or a parent.

There is another aspect to Hollywood which is soul destroying. It perhaps began with the play acting of the pagans, especially the Greeks. Later it was developed into a fine art in England by men such as Chaucer, Marlow and Shakespeare. It also was fostered by the romantic novels of the last three centuries. These developed a wholly unrealistic view of marriage—a view often built upon most impractical and unrealistic expectations of the marriage partner and portraying a glamour far from the realities of everyday life. Especially in young ladies, it led to daydreaming which led to expectations which would easily lead to disillusionment with the realities of marriage responsibilities.

Young people, you have a choice to behold Christ or to behold evil. The choice you make will greatly impact the success of your marriage and its enduring stability. If your mind is regularly filled with evil you will view divorce in a wholly different perspective from that expectation which results when your mind is filled by daily communion with Christ.

18

Other Risk Factors

IN reviewing some of the most common practices which predispose the
marriage couple to subsequent divorce, we are not suggesting that we
are presenting a comprehensive list, neither are we suggesting that these
practices are necessarily presented in order of their importance. Obviously,
most divorces are more than single-issue situations. Clearly, there are frequently a multiplicity of factors, of which some are not within the control
of the persons themselves. One factor beyond the control of the marriage
partners is the effect of having divorced parents. In the chapter entitled "Divorce in the United States" the statistics revealed that those from broken
homes divorced at the rate of forty-three percent in the first ten years of
marriage. Wives whose parents had remained married divorced at the considerably lower rate of twenty-nine percent in the first ten years.

While a stable home background is not a guarantee that the children will
have a stable marriage of their own, yet they do have a great advantage in
that most young people have learned to model the principles of their parents. We must never forget that children learn much more effectively by
example than by precept. If the parents are unstable, insecure, poorly ad-
justed and erratic in their behavior, there is a much greater likelihood that
their children will follow in the same direction.

The Word of God gives significant indications of this inconstancy in
the second commandment,

> Thou shalt not make unto thee any graven image, or any likeness of any thing
> that is in heaven above, or that is in the earth beneath, or that is in the water
> under the earth: Thou shalt not bow down thyself to them, nor serve them: for I
> the Lord thy God am a jealous God, visiting the iniquity of the fathers upon the
> children unto the third and fourth generation of them that hate me.
>
> Exodus 20:4–5

There is no question that the training of the child from his experience in
the womb is essential for all areas of life, including a successful marriage.
Of course none of us had control over our prenatal environment. That is
largely the responsibility of our parents, especially the mother. Every child

needs to be trained in self-control, and that begins in the womb. The truly Christian mother will not indulge her own passions, appetites or emotions. She will ever be mindful of the necessity of a simple and quiet environment for the developing child in her womb. Of course, the father has significant responsibilities in doing what he can to make the life of the expectant mother as emotionally stable as possible. The embryo and fetus are vulnerable to almost every kind of influence. If both mother and father are under the influence of the Holy Spirit, then automatically the child is under that influence. This is very well defined in the experience of John the Baptist, who was filled with the Holy Ghost from his mother's womb.

. . . and he shall be filled with the Holy Ghost, even from his mother's womb.
Luke 1:15

His mother was filled with the Holy Spirit,

. . . and Elizabeth was filled with the Holy Ghost. Luke 1:41

Later his father was filled with the Holy Spirit.

And his father Zacharias was filled with the Holy Ghost, and prophesied.
Luke 1:67

What a blessing to the fetus and infant!

Very important in the prenatal training of the child is the emotional stability of the mother. If the mother is quickly and easily upset and experiences many emotional upheavals, this will have a negative effect upon the development of the child and will impact upon the child's own later emotional stability. It must ever be remembered that negative emotions generate the production of adrenalin, which enters the blood stream, some of which passes into the fetus' blood via the placenta.

The food and liquids which are ingested by the mother are also important. Food additives are frequently stimulants; coffee, tea and cola drinks are stimulants; as are other junk foods and drinks. The danger of indiscipline later has much to do with the prenatal environment, and consequently has a significant effect upon the stability, or lack thereof, of the offspring. Good prenatal as well as postnatal environment and upbringing are invaluable to a good, stable and enduring marriage.

Now let us address issues which are more relevant to the individual and can come under the control of that individual.

1. Marrying young

The younger the couple are at marriage, the greater the likelihood of instability, therefore the greater the risk of divorce. We in the western world are living in an extraordinarily complicated age. Rather than marriages being contracted at an early age, they should be contracted much later than in former generations. Simple societies are quite different from sophisticated societies. Yet in every society there are important priorities before engaging in marriage. Keep in mind that before even the thought of marriage should enter the mind of young men or women, they must first search their own hearts to make sure that they have surrendered their lives to Christ. This is the essential building block of all other maturities. These counsels are not meant in any way to condone living in common-law relationships; this call is for responsible restraint.

Sadly, in the western world there is a rapid decline in interest in Christian commitment. Yet to the earnest young man or woman this step will be the first and timely priority. Second, there is the issue of future ability in the work place. Of course, the first question which Christians raise will be the submissive words of Paul, "Lord, what wilt thou have me to do?" (Acts 9:6). No matter what the calling we undertake, our first responsibility is to be of service and witness to Jesus Christ. Therefore the reaction and preparation for a life calling is most important. So many today change occupations multiple times during their adult life. Of course, with the rapid change in technology and other such societal conditions, sometimes a change and retraining will be necessary. However, change is always a difficult time for any individual. The most successful individuals will be those who have a lifelong occupation for a profession or career. Life is far more predictable this way. No one should enter marriage until such a time as they have a stable income. This is especially important to the man who is the primary provider for his wife and future family. Third, he should be determined to show himself responsible in the work place. Irresponsibility or discontent in the work place is a very poor foundation for a stable married life. Thus it is that early marriages are more vulnerable to divorce than those in which the couple have matured into stable adults before seeking the heavy responsibilities of matrimony.

2. Lack of Common Interests

Another factor which leads to divorce is lack of common interests in the lives of the newlyweds. This may not seem so important in the courting situation, especially as often it is the attractiveness of physical features which drives the relationship. However, as time erodes the physical aspects of marriage, common interests are a very important glue to the marriage. It can be most frustrating when the interests of marriage partners are far different from each other. This situation can precipitate the spouses looking in other directions for new interests in the opposite sex among those with whom they share common interests.

3. Financial Responsibility

Financial crises can lead to most stressful circumstances in marriage. Not always are such crises the result of circumstances beyond the control of the marriage partners. Some spouses are very irresponsible in the use of money and never seem to seek a way to live within their means. This has been exacerbated by the ability to accumulate many credit cards, and for one or both of the spouses to use them irresponsibly; and therefore this practice inevitably leads to great concerns in the marriage, and often to the placing of blame upon one or other of the spouses. Combative argumentations become frequent and mutual love rapidly ebbs away. Not uncommonly, debt is a big contributor to the breakdown of the marriage. Sometimes irresponsible debt leads one spouse to take legal action to protect against his or her responsibility for the debts of the other spouse. If in a marriage one spouse is responsible financially and the other is not, then surely it should be the responsible spouse who is entrusted with the financial affairs of the household. However, even this arrangement can cause great stress, as the one who is irresponsible becomes angry at the tight controls of the other on the purse strings. Thus the financially responsible spouse should not be unbearably tight-fisted, but fair and reasonable to the one he/she loves.

4. Different Religious Value Systems

Scripture is very plain that Christians should not be unequally yoked together with unbelievers, as we have previously shown.

> Be ye not unequally yoked together with unbelievers: for what fellowship hath righteousness with unrighteousness? and what communion hath light with darkness.   2 Corinthians 6:14

This precaution normally includes those of different religious faiths. Such a marriage can cause great difficulties, especially when children are born. Often there results a tug-of-war between the father and the mother as to what religious teachings the children will receive and to which churches they will attend. Recently Colin met a Roman Catholic man who married an Anglican wife. The wife suggested that their marriage be conducted by two priests—one from each church. The husband-to-be refused, and settled the issue by deciding that the Roman Catholic priest would perform the marriage. However, not so readily understood is the fact that such a test can also apply to those who are of the same religious affiliation, but when there is a deep chasm between the dedication and commitment of one compared with the other. Once again, the value systems, even though the couple belong to the same church, may be substantially different, and this can lead to great strain upon the marriage. Wise young people will ever seek to marry only one who shares the same religious convictions and value systems, and as a consequence they will largely eliminate the stress not only upon the marriage partners but also upon the children initiated into the family.

5. Poor Communications

When one spouse proves to be a poor communicator, this factor can lead to great frustration for the other. Often a spouse holds secrets from the other spouse which certainly are appropriate to be shared. Some persons seem incompetent in presenting their own desires and judgments, and when the spouse moves in other directions they become extremely agitated, sometimes leading to estrangement from each other. This is especially likely if the partners are moody. Sometimes one spouse does not know how to relate to the other, not knowing whether he or she will be reclusive or more communicative. Once again, great difficulties may result. There are spouses who consistently refuse to dialogue with the other spouse on different beliefs, perspectives or family matters. Once again this can lead to alienation in the marriage. It is exceedingly important, where there are differences, that both spouses can sit down and calmly and openly discuss those differences. Usually, open communication is the best avenue for resolving tensions within the home. This dictum applies not only to openness between the spouses but also to communication with the children. Closed communication leads to uncertainty and unhappiness, even suspicion, and can challenge the security of the marriage.

6. Self Centeredness

Self-centered persons are very difficult spouses with whom to live. Their selfishness can create great anguish to the other spouse. When a husband loves his wife and he seeks to please her more than to please himself and when a wife loves her husband and seeks to serve and please him more than herself, there is almost inevitably an excellent marriage. It is also a great example to the children in the family.

7. Influence of the Media

We must not underestimate the influence of the media upon the dissatisfaction of some spouses in the marriage. The media, especially the television and the worldwide web, present values and practices which are wholly inimical to a happy Christian marriage. Just like novel reading in the past caused many women to be dissatisfied with their married life, so television in the modern age can cause similar dissatisfaction both for the husband and the wife. The media inevitably presents a view of marriage which is quite contrary to divine principles and conducive to marital infidelity. Wise Christians will either avoid television altogether or, alternatively, choose only very limited programming which is edifying and informative. Few succeed in making this distinction..

8. Preparation for Marriage

The preparation for marriage should not be rushed. Every effort should be made to seek to know the other person over a period of time without allowing the emotions to take control. Marriage is too serious a step in life to be built almost entirely upon emotions. Careful evaluation and observations need to be made. It is never wise for a young man or woman to play on the affections of another individual without the most careful pre-courtship evaluations. When this is done there is much less hurt if a separation has to be made. Too much is at stake for anything short of careful, prayerful evaluation to guide the pre-courtship period. Rushed marriages often lead to rushed divorces.

9. Addictions

Wisdom dictates that no Christian marry an individual with addictions. Addictions include street drugs, alcohol, tobacco. Even caffeine drinks which, while milder than other drugs, have a significant negative effect upon the emotions. However, there are other addictions which also need to be avoided. Some such addictions include gambling, sports, or worldly entertainment. Such addictions can also be devastating to a marriage. They can lead to serious consequences in the marriage. No true Christian will follow such destructive addictions.

A young, miserable-looking woman, already unattractive at the age of twenty-eight, entered Russell's medical clinic. Her request was simple, "All I want is some Valium [a sedative] to calm me down. Russell could have complied in a few moments and increased his bank account with little effort. But such professional irresponsibility would have been reprehensible.

Seeking to assist this poor woman, Russell inquired as to the source of the need for Valium. The woman replied, "I can't control my irritation, I'm screaming at my husband and my two kids all the time. I love my husband, but I think he's going to leave me. All I need is Valium to calm me down."

Seeking to explore the problem in this young married woman's life, Russell questioned if any external things in her life aggravated her problem. "No, I'm just like it all the time," was her rather irritated response.

However, after a brief pause this distressed young lady solved her own problem. "Oh, I suppose I feel a bit better after a cup of coffee, but not much." Her words in this last moment of reflection was the solution to her problem. We hasten to state that the solution did not lie in suggesting that she imbibe more caffeine.

Russell casually inquired, "How many cups of coffee do you drink each day?" She replied revealingly, "Oh, I don't know, I don't bother to count every cup I drink. Some days I suppose I might drink thirteen or fifteen." Here lay the solution to her marriage-destroying behavior.

Caffeine is no minor drug. It is unfit for our bodies whether consumed in tea, coffee or cola drinks or any other form. An average cup of tea or coffee contains around one hundred milligrams of caffeine, which has a profound stimulating and irritating effect upon the entire nervous system including the brain.

Russell concluded that this young woman was suffering from caffeine toxicity. He encouragingly told the patient that he believed he could solve her problem, but that the course of treatment would be difficult.

The patient replied, "I'll do anything to get better!" Brave and desperate words were these. However in a few seconds Russell discovered, to his great disappointment, that she had overstated her promise. Most assuredly she would NOT do anything, for she utterly refused to undertake the sole solution available for the problem.

Russell simply told her to cease all coffee, tea and cola drinks. The woman exploded. "You want me to go mad, don't you? You'll put me in a mental asylum and destroy my marriage. I came here to get Valium, not to listen to your stupid advice." As she stormed out of Russell's clinic, she shouted back, "I've wasted my money coming to see you."

Russell suspected she could find a doctor in the vicinity who would provide her with false hopes by writing a prescription for Valium. After this unprecedented altercation in Russell's experience as an internist (specialist physician), Russell mentally expressed surprise that her husband was still residing with her. Russell had experienced a dose of the venom of her tongue, which by her own admission was a daily event in the lives of her husband and children.

Earlier in the interview Russell had asked the patient if the family had financial worries or if she was enduring problems with her in-laws. Her answers had been in the negative to both these questions. Irritated by his probing, she sharply responded to Russell, "It's no use, it is just the way I am, I've been like this for a long time, at least for ten years."

Russell soon forgot the patient after thanking God that he had not married someone like that. One does not choose to ponder on his failures as a physician. Russell felt certain that this was one patient he would never see again.

Three or four months later an attractive woman was ushered into

Russell's office. He had no recollection of ever seeing her previously. However, when he looked down at the patient's card, he noticed a previous record of consultation in his own handwriting. This confrontational patient had incredibly returned!

Looking into her eyes, Russell said, "I'm surprised to see you again. I had written on this card, 'Patient rejected advice and does not intend to return.'"

Frankly, she stated that that comment accurately reflected her intention.

"How can I help you?" Russell questioned. Her reply was as surprising and as sweet as her transformed appearance. "I've just come to thank you!" Russell has over the years received many expressions of appreciation through letters or telephone conversations or when returning with further problems or check-ups, but this lady stands out as his lone patient when returned to his clinic, to say a word of gratitude, requiring no medical assistance. Russell was deeply touched.

"What caused you to accept my advice to cease drinking caffeine beverages?" Russell inquired. She related her story. She was furious when she returned home. She told him she was too embarrassed to reveal to him the words she shouted back to her husband evaluating Russell's perceived lack of medical skills, in response to her desperate husband's simple question, "What did the doctor say?" But she did mention my "stupid" advice.

The level of the husband's desperation may be measured by the fact that he made no verbal response to his wife. He silently went to the kitchen pantry, took out the jar of coffee and the tea-bags and silently dropped the contents into the trash can. Turning to his wife he commanded her, "And don't you dare buy any more!"

The woman thought she was going insane over the next five days as she endured severe withdrawal symptoms of caffeine addiction. Then little by little she discovered that she was a normal, caring wife and mother after all. Russell trusts that her husband and her children enjoyed the love of his attractive wife ever after.

Russell did not meet this woman again. Her case illustrates just how dangerous caffeine is. We never drink caffeine drinks for we believe that they are inconsistent with a Christian lifestyle. Yet at many church functions today these beverages are frequently offered.

Many persons drinking far less coffee or tea than the patient described above, are nevertheless destroying their characters by thus doing. If we love our spouses and children and desire a God-ordained happy and loving marriage, we must not defile ourselves with such drugs. This is our God-ordained duty.

There are other behaviors which take place before marriage which also contribute to the heightened risk of divorce:

a. Familiarity and frivolity with the opposite sex is rampant today, but it is a poor preparation for marriage. Young ladies should keep a womanly reserve to separate themselves from careless behavior with, and in the presence of, those of the opposite sex. Young men should learn early to respect members of the opposite sex. They have a responsibility not to trivialize their communications with young ladies, for this often translates into a lack of respect in the married life. This, of course, does not prohibit happy, relaxed conversations with young ladies, but it totally requires that young men should refrain from lewd and suggestive remarks or actions.

Other forms of familiarity, such as touching and putting arms around each other, again is a form of behavior which can easily translate into continuing the same behavior with the opposite sex after marriage. Such behavior is very provocative and often sexually stimulating and very harmful to marriage, and therefore should not be practiced as a preparation for marriage.

b. Common worldly wisdom encourages young people to "date around with quite a number of those of the opposite sex." This worldly wisdom claims that this conduct is a valid and wise preparation for marriage. After all, how can young people learn the characteristics of those of the opposite sex which appeal to them if they have not explored this kind of experience. However there are lifelong dangers in these multiple flirtations. So often young men whisper "sweet nothings" in the ear of a young lady, raising emotional expectations on the part of the young lady, only to see those expectations dashed, causing strain, stress and disappointment. It is a fearful thing to trifle with the emotions of another human being. No such behavior honors God nor leads to godly respect for members of the opposite sex.

The greatest danger of "dating about" is that misbehavior develops habits, habits which are not easily broken. Young men and women learn to crave the attention which comes from multiple members of the opposite sex paying attention to them. The young men, especially, take delight in the number of women who are willing to accept the invitation to "come out with them," or to "have a date with them." Therefore many young men and not a few young women have familiarity with scores of members of the opposite sex prior to marriage. They have a certain level of reinforcement and gratification as a result of this. When eventually they are standing at the altar vowing to love, cherish, honor the one who is standing with them at the altar, they hardly know their own hearts and characters for it is so easy to carry on the habit of flirtation after marriage, for this habit has become very attractive to them. Fearful marital problems can result and lead to infidelity and broken homes.

c. Premarital Sex

The common wisdom of many is the crude "try before you buy" philosophy. Marriage is seriously trivialized when it is compared to something akin to buying clothing. Surely you would not buy a dress or a suit without trying it on first. Under this faulty reasoning, many young people give themselves over to fornication and licentiousness. Once again, this becomes the habit of their lives. Rather than such behavior helping to develop a stable marriage, it is all in the other direction. Such faulted thinking will lead to unstable marriages, and even if that premarital sex has been with the one who will become your life partner, it is still very unwise. Many times it has led to the conception of a child. Often this is handled by abortion or, by the time the child is born, the young man who has been responsible for the child has long since deserted the young lady involved. Such circumstances will never provide the confidence in marriage which would grow if both spouses go to the altar pure. There are far fewer divorces among those who have maintained moral integrity prior to marriage than among those who have participated in sexual activity before marriage. The more times fornication occurs, especially with multiple partners, the greater the likelihood of failure of the marriage.

d. Pornography

Many men, especially, and also some women, are addicted to pornography. The access to pornography on web sites has only exacerbated the number of undisciplined and sensual individuals who develop such an addiction.

> Whosoever looketh on a woman to lust after her hath committed adultery with her already in his heart. Matthew 5:28

Sadly, many of those proceeding toward marriage already have vile and corrupted minds. Once again, such a one is a very poor prospect for marriage. Not that God cannot forgive, not that God cannot give the power to overcome, but the risks are great unless there be a total transformation of the life through sincere repentance and commitment to God. Even then, from time to time, Satan will fiercely tempt the individual upon those weaknesses he or she has experienced in early life.

e. Homosexuality and Lesbianism

Many men or women have married without any knowledge that the one whom they have married has entered into covert homosexual or lesbian activities. What a shock it is when the husband or wife begins to question whether the other one is directed towards those of the same sex. It is not uncommon for men or women with homosexual directions in their lives to marry in the hope that somehow marriage will help them to gain heterosexual orientations. However, it is only God who has the power to help the homosexual. Merely marrying does not change anything; and the perversion leads to problems in the marriage, and is frequently a forerunner of divorce.

f. Children of Divorced Parents

Another impediment to a happy marriage, and one which predisposes husbands and wives to divorce, includes having come from homes where their parents have divorced. Of course, this factor is not in the control of the children. However it is a factor which needs to be taken very seriously, and which should lead to very deep reflection. How important it is for those who are from dysfunctional homes or divorced homes themselves, to prepare carefully by studying God's counsel concerning preparation for marriage. There is great blessing to be gained by also talking with Christians who have a very strong marriage. They can give excellent advice.

g. Working Wives

There is much evidence that women who are in the regular work force are more likely to divorce than those who become full-time homemakers and who care for and train their children. In the work force women meet attractive men, and they themselves are often pursued. It is not uncommon, for example, for a secretary to be pursued by the boss for whom she is working. Sadly, some of the women yield to this temptation, thus increasing the risk of the breakup of their own marriage.

h. Physical Abuse

Men, and occasionally women, become quite physically abusive, often of their spouse, and sometimes of their children, or both. Those who practice physical abuse tend to become more violent as the years pass by, to the point that sometimes even the partner's life is in danger. It is a most disgusting situation. Often if a man comes from a home where his own father has been physically abusive, he himself will follow the same pattern in his marriage. Yet this need not be if the man learns from the misery of his mother.

We cannot recommend a wife continuing to stay with a man who cowardly takes advantage of his superior strength. This is also the case if he is physically abusing his own children. Any individual who wins disputes on the basis of his physical superiority is a man lacking in virtue, love and common decency. For protective purposes the wife, with her children, may need to separate from such a husband. However, we must remember that such a wife does not have biblical grounds for remarriage.

i. Sexual Abuse

Sexual abuse is a growingly frequent cause of marital breakup. Many lustful men take great liberties in the marriage situation. While sexual relations are a normal and God-given privilege in the marriage bond, this does not include seeking to force wives into deviant and abnormal sexual practices. Tragically, many men seek to take advantage of their children in incestuous relationships. Unfortunately, many wives either are blind to such activities or they do nothing to protect their children. Wives must not permit such activities to continue, and if there be no change, then it is essential that the wife move the children where they are no longer ravished by their own father. Occasionally women also practice such incestuous relationships. That is just as wicked as if the father is responsible. Obviously these practices can lead to divorce, and in such a case the spouse does have grounds for remarriage, for the perpetrator has violated the solemn, sacred vows of marriage.

j. Verbal Abuse

Verbal abuse is an area much more difficult to define. What might be felt to be verbal abuse by one spouse may not reach to that level in the mind of another. However, if we follow the principles of heaven there will be kindness and understanding between husband and wife and children even when there are disagreements. Many women feel demeaned and belittled by their husbands. Some husbands develop the habit of speaking derogatively of their wives to others. Such men are breaking their marriage vow. Women who do the same concerning their husband likewise break the marriage vow. God expects us constantly to express our thoughts in words of tenderness and love. When verbal abuse becomes habitual, clearly, the marriage is vulnerable, and sometimes this will lead to divorce. Many women are culpable in this area, browbeating and berating loving and doting husbands to the point of emasculating them.

Young people contemplating marriage need to understand the character of the other person before they marry. If they behave in patterns which are consistent with some of the above characteristics, it is better, far better to break the relationship and wait for a more worthy person to enter your life. Young people should not quickly put aside the warnings of their parents if the parents bring to their attention characteristics in the suitor which are not likely to be an indication of a future happy marriage. Ultimately, only when both spouses are dedicated Christians can we expect an invincible marriage.

19

Consequences for Children of the Divorced

IT would seem that rarely do parents comprehensively consider all the consequences of divorce. Of course it is difficult to know what the outcomes will be even for the spouses, let alone the children. For example, would parents divorce if they knew the divorce would lead to a frustrated child or would lead the child into a life of crime, maybe even murder? Would they divorce if they knew that such a child would battle long term mental illness? Would they divorce if they knew the child would commit suicide as a result of the divorce? Yet these are not uncommon consequences. When such tragedies take place, it might well be that the parents will be in denial, but their self-motivated actions leading to divorce were pivotal to the child's maladaptive behavior. Sometimes parents who have had rocky marriages, yet have sufficient maturity and responsibility to maintain the home for the benefit of the children, have made by far the wiser decision.

Even when the children are grown, the consequences of divorce can be severe. Colin recently encountered a family where the parents, on the verge of divorce, wisely decided to dialogue with their grown unmarried children. The children were open enough to express their deep desire for the parents to remain together and, by the grace of God, they did. The parents listened and made a new commitment to each other which seemed to bring new life to the shaky marriage. The parents both realized that they still had love for each other.

On the other hand, one happily married young man expressed the view, following the divorce of his parents, that he could never imagine the breakup of his parents' marriage being more shattering for him, at any earlier stage of his life.

Let us explore the tragic consequences of breaking up a lifelong commitment.

1. Who can predict the lives of children subsequent to the divorce of the parents? Can one spouse provide a better family environment than two parents? Would the children be better with the grandparents? However, what if the grandparents are themselves divorced or sickly or incapacitated? Would they be better off as wards of the state or in foster home care? How satisfying is it to be provided only limited access to your own children? What if the parent with family custody of the children moves far away from the other parent?

2. What sadness and frustration results when one of the spouses has little day-to-day knowledge of his or her own children and their lives, their character development, their challenges, their school life, and other essential aspects that are important to caring parents.

3. So often in split families, one or both parents are subtly, or not so subtly, seeking to gain a greater love and loyalty from the children beyond that of the other parent. This is especially tempting to parents when custody battles are ensuing before the courts. It has been greatly intensified now when these custody battles take place by the time the children are still minors in their teenage years. Judges are inclined to take seriously the desires of the children. This naturally leads to strong efforts to "bribe" the children so as to gain a positive report in their testimony before the judge.

However this "bribing" is not limited to custody battles. It commonly occurs even when one party has only limited visitation rights. It has a serious impact upon the character development of the children for such "bribing" is never benign in its impact upon the child. It tends to impede greatly the character development of the child for with rare exception the "bribe" panders to the carnal desires of the children at the very time of life when the children need firm guidance as they are growing towards the time when they themselves will be firming their characters as they develop toward adulthood.

All too often do children of divorced parents favor the more permissive parent. This could have eternal consequences. Such "bribery" often paralyzes the efforts of the godly spouse in seeking the Christian training of the children. Unfortunately, the children in such custody battles have only in the rarest cases made their decision for Christ. We must keep in mind that many judges today operate on the principle of majoritarianism, by which they will favor the spouse whose values and practices are closest to the permissive practices of mainstream contemporary society.

Russell recalls a fellow missionary physician serving in the Far East, whom he encountered at meetings once or twice. On his return to his homeland, the United States, his womanizing ways surfaced. He left his devoted and dutiful wife, a woman of high principles, in the process alienating his teenage son and daughter from their mother by painting her to them as a nagging mother when, in love, this dear mother was simply placing the standards of the character of Christ before them.

This lady was an only child. Both of her parents were dead. This disgraceful physician deprived her of all that remained in her life—her children, whom the father led into lives of sin similar to his own infidelity.

Her life systematically shattered by her wicked husband, she died at her own hand, so unloved, so uncared for, that although she was living in what was essentially a community of Christians, her body was not found until a considerable time had passed after her death.

4. Sometimes children appear to have been minimally affected by the divorce. Occasionally a parent is heard to say something like this, "My children are handling the divorce with little effect upon their lives." Maybe their studies do not seem to be affected. Their pattern of life seemed little changed. But sometimes the parent is expressing what he or she hopes is the outcome, rather than the reality of the stresses and ravages of competing loyalties in the minds of the children. The expressions of words and actions do not always tell the whole story. With some children their emotions and thoughts run very deep. They may not be as adaptable as they appear to be on the surface. There may still be serious emotional scarring. The effects of divorce may be life-long, ultimately influencing the children's own marriages and their own ability to parent wisely.

5. Parents, do not forget the effect upon your children in the events which lead up to your divorce. The children can be plunged into the deepest insecurity and uncertainty. Often their minds are plagued with fears and hopes. Sometimes it appears that the marriage is about to be over, although they may have reason to hope that the marriage will survive. Sometimes the spouse leaves the home, then decides to give the marriage "another chance" which can happen a number of times, creating a roller-coaster ride for the emotions of the children.

6. So often before, during and after the divorce, the children's minds are bombarded with revelations of the faults of the other parent. At times both parents battle this way for the loyalty of the children. In the end it is easy for the children to lose all respect for both their parents. If one of the parents is engaged in this wretched practice, it is our observation that the parent involved is at least as likely to lose the loyalty of the children, and thus they fail to achieve the goal of weakening the children's loyalty and love for the other parent. Indeed, sometimes the children become even more protective of the other parent whom they love.

7. When one parent remarries it can be another dagger in the heart of the children, for it usually signals the finish of even the last lingering hopes that the marriage can be reestablished. It can also create serious insecurities in the minds of the children because there is frequently great resentment. When the divorce occurred early in the lives of the children and there has been an extended period of time before the custodial parent has remarried, often the step-parent is seen as an intruder into the life of the children, robbing them of the exclusive love of that parent. The new spouse occupies much of the time with their mother, or their father, which was once focused upon the children.

Further, the new spouse can resent the children, especially when their behavior irritates him or her or when the genetic parent becomes over-protective of the children. This is not to ignore the fact that the same reaction may result from the remarriage of a parent who has lost a spouse in death. Nor do we ignore the fact that sometimes step-parents have provided a good substitute for the parent who has left the marriage. Indeed, some have been very godly influences, much superior to the genetic parent.

8. Remarriages can be very much complicated by both spouses bringing children into the new marriage. Even greater complications can develop when children are born into the new marriage. When there are "your children, my children and our children," the very different dispositions, characters and activities of the mixed families can prove to be a very great test for both spouses of the second and any subsequent marriages.

9. Keep in mind that a second marriage for one or both spouses is more likely to break apart than a first marriage. This results from a number of factors, not the least being the psychological factor that the first divorce is usually most difficult and painful. Once divorce has taken place it seems a less shameful or distressing step to break up another marriage. Colin has concluded, from his experience, that when a divorced person has remarried to a spouse who has not been previously married and this marriage is in trouble, it is more likely to be the previously married spouse who is desirous of the divorce, and it is the spouse in his or her first marriage who works harder to save the marriage. Multiple divorces and remarriages have a most destabilizing effect upon the children, beside setting an example which can greatly herald disastrous marriages in the future for these children. Neither should we ignore the results of such an unstable life upon the experience of the man or woman who has been in and out of marriage a number of times.

10.   In some separations and divorces, one child lives with one parent and another with the other parent. This may be the preference of the children or may be the mutual agreement of the parents. We again count the effects this has upon the children, for it is usually naturally beneficial for children to grow up together as a family. Although it is not uncommon for children to develop sibling rivalry, yet it is advantageous to learn to live appropriately with others of a similar age. Usually, when such a decision is made, the boys go with the father and the girls with the mother. This robs the boys and girls of the modeling of members of the opposite sex which can be so helpful to the understanding in the choice of a spouse. Of course in this time of small families in the western world, many families will have children of only one sex. If in rare cases the girls are with the father and boys with the mother, it is an even more hazardous arrangement, for it can increase the possibility of the girls becoming lesbians and the boys homosexuals because they are deprived the good modeling of their own sex. This consequence, of course, is far from inevitable.

11.   Many times one spouse, usually the wife, feels that the children are better off without the other. Yet most times this is not the case. However we do hasten to add this is usually best in most cases of sexual abuse or severe physical abuse. This decision has to be very carefully made—for every factor must be weighed objectively and with only one issue uppermost: the good of the family, not the selfish desires of the spouses. We repeat that though a spouse may be far from perfect, data reveals that it takes an extraordinarily bad or nonfunctional parent to justify the likely consequences upon the children of a divorce.

12.   The consequences upon the children, especially in the case of a deserted wife, can be devastating. Sadly, in today's society, there are many men who desert the family and provide no form of support for wives or children, and in one way or another they separate themselves from the reach of the law. This often forces the family into the social system for financial support, or they become dependant upon the financial support of family, friends or fellow church members. It often happens that the wife is forced into the work place, frequently in low paying positions, and she is faced sometimes with the need to work in a second, or occasionally even a third job, simply to support the family. Thus the deserted wife has little time left to be a mother, and the children are terribly neglected and removed from a stable upbringing, so that they are often slaves of their uncontrolled home life and are easy prey for Satan. Even if circumstances do not place the mother in strait financial circumstances, yet the desertion by a father brings inordinate pressure upon the divorced mother, whose task is most difficult in today's wicked society.

13.   Children growing up in a one-parent home sometime become the obsession of that parent. The desertion of a parent not infrequently results in the feelings of failure and inadequacies. The craving for love and acceptance occupies the mind. Thus such a one, to a greater or lesser extent, establishes his or her self worth, not on what God did for the human race and the sacrifice and love of Jesus, but upon the measure of human approbation. Therefore the inordinate focus of winning the love of the children often leads to the desire to please the children's every whim, resulting in severe negative consequences.

Colin was approached by a mother who suffered from this exact situation when she was a child. She explained that when she was two years old her father left her mother. As the only child, the mother had placed all her attention upon this daughter. She became the single-minded focus of this mother. She could not remember her mother ever saying, "No." Now, when Colin met her, she was the wife of a man training for the gospel ministry. Her great frustration was that now she had no skill in disciplining her children. She had to leave all the discipline to her husband—a most difficult situation. Thus she felt a terrible void in handling her two little children. Far reaching are the consequences of breaking up a home.

14.   Finally, but not exhaustively, there is the situation of a divorced parent consenting to live in a non-binding, common-law, unmarried state with a new partner, which is frequent in today's amoral society. What a tragic example to the children! What does all this portend for succeeding generations? What a decision marriage is! How careful must be this decision! How important it is to be wholly under the guidance of the Lord before considering marriage and how carefully must young people today seek marriage. They should consider marriage only after becoming certain that the one they ask to marry them, or the one who consents to marry, is also fully converted and under the direction of God.

15.   It is common for the children of a divorce to develop deep depression and serious behavioral and abnormal social problems. Studies have also shown that,

a.   There is in some cases, the development of bed wetting, nightmares, withdrawal from normal communications, aggressiveness and excessive sleep.

b.   Such children exhibit confusion and, in detailing the events which have taken place, will often tell different versions inconsistent with previous versions of the same situation.

c.   Children of divorced parents often find it very difficult to make and attract friends because they feel so insecure and "different" from other children who have a stable home.

d.   The children of divorced parents who have deep, enduring insecurity are far more likely to engage in early sex—girls are moved by the desire for acceptance, boys so as to prove that they can be successful in wooing the "love" of the opposite sex.

e.   Often the children are left with a mother who has the sole responsibility in discipline. Frequently, especially as the children reach towards the rebellious teenage years, the disciplinary authority of the mother is challenged, often ignored, and this leads to great tension and often to violent arguments.

f.   Many children experience feelings of great shame when their parents are divorced, or even separated, and this will accentuate feelings of insecurity and rejection.

g.   Very frequently divorce leads to a significant decrease in the scholastic performance of the children.

h.   In a formerly well-adjusted child, change can take place rapidly and decisively: the child may become moody, sullen, aggressive, suicidal, homicidal, and is much more likely to join gangs.

i.   Divorce can drive children to immature and dangerous independence.

j.   Children of divorce frequently feel betrayed by the divorcing parents and are much more likely to believe their parents do not love them.

k.   It is much more common for youth of divorce to distance themselves from the home. They normally absent themselves to avoid the painful trauma of which their home reminds them.

l.   Sometimes one or both of the parents become so involved with new romantic interests that they spare little time for their children. This exacerbates the feeling by the children that they are not loved, and that home is an undesirable place to be.

m.   Children of divorced parents are more likely to marry young, and young marriages are frequently in themselves irresponsible marriages.

20

Mothers Sacrificing Careers

TODAY there is an increasing trend in the United States for mothers to sacrifice their careers for the benefit of their children. The cover story in *Time* magazine, March 22, 2004, was captioned "The Case for Staying Home." It was subtitled, "Why More Mums are Opting Out of the Rat Race." The article pointed out that "dual career couples with children under eighteen had combined work hours of eighty-one a week in 1977. In 2002 the average had grown to ninety-one." The article also stated that even if a parent opts to work from home, often the day is so punctuated with telephone calls, e-mails, faxes, or other forms of communication that the time with the children becomes very disrupted, and therefore the parental care is inadequate for the children.

Presently, seventy-two percent of mothers with children under eighteen are in the work force. The increase is from forty-seven percent in 1975. These family-career homes care for their children in different ways. Many use day-care centers; others employ nannies to come to the home to care for the children; while still others have relatives, frequently grandparents, who care for the children (*Ibid.*). In these arrangements children are likely to have very little communication with their parents. There is a fragility in the bonding of these children with their parents. The situation also leads to little communication between parents. All these things contribute to the likelihood of the fractionation of the family circle, and can easily drift toward separation and divorce.

The *Time* article, however, gives this encouragement, citing evidence that there has been a drop-off in work place participation by married mothers with a child less than one year old. The figure "fell from fifty-nine percent in 1997 to fifty-three percent in 2000." The article pointed out that the significant drop was mainly with women who were white, over thirty and well educated. Many factors are clashing in these situations. Women are far more likely to be highly educated today than they were in any previous generation. Many have high qualifications in professional areas and in the business field. Often marriage is delayed, and further, the decision to have a first child is delayed. Therefore the women have often worked for a considerable number of years and achieved considerable seniority in their position, and thus they are often on the brink of appointment to senior administrative roles with high, or potentially high, incomes just around the corner. It is at this very time that such a mother has to make a decision. Will she choose her promising career in her most critical years of progress and upward mobility, or will she put the interest of her child or children first? That many mothers are choosing their children over careers, is shown in the estimates of home-schooled children in the United States, now approximately two million, up from about half a million twenty-five years ago.

Typical of such a decision was that made by a woman serving in the business office of a college where Colin served as president. The business manager asserted that she was his most valued associate. However, she decided to resign to care for her two-year-old boy. When Colin conducted an exit interview with her, she said that over the weekend her husband and she had prayerfully decided that it was more important for their son to have a mother at home than carpet on the floor of their home, or other home conveniences which they once had thought essential. Colin fully gave his assurances that she was doing the right thing.

This consumer-driven society strongly tempts the well trained mother to lift her financial security and standards of living to a level which rarely can be maintained on a one-spouse salary. Further, often with the bright financial prospects of both spouses the family has gone deeply into debt for homes, luxury cars and other upscale purchases. Many today face challenges, especially for those high-octane spouses, which make choices very difficult. If the career is chosen, undoubtedly the children will suffer greatly. It is tragic for children to grow up hardly knowing their parents, and indeed to be far more bonded to daycare personnel, skilled teachers, grandparents and others with whom they may be entrusted by the parents. This only exacerbates the likely challenges in the teen-age years, as the children do not have that closeness, and that bonding with parents which once was so common in society. The family which makes the decision for the mother to render up her occupation brings her so much satisfaction in the caring for her children. Such a mother is indeed following principles which will greatly enhance the physical, emotional, social, intellectual and spiritual lives of the children. Such a decision is made difficult today because many husbands are earning salaries well below that of their wives. This makes the decision for the wife more challenging. Some may need to sacrifice to pay off debt so that the family can live on a one-spouse income.

When the husband's salary will not cover the mortgages and other payments which have become part of the lifestyle of the family, in some cases decisions are made in which the husband decides that he will surrender his occupation and allow the wife to continue. This is rarely a good solution. First, few fathers can provide the same wonderful care for their children as the mother. There is no question that in the Christian family, the husband should be the primary bread-winner and supporter of his family. Much is lost when the roles are reversed, and there may be great social and psychological implications for the children.

Once again, we would reiterate that it is far, far better for families to sacrifice financially so that the mother can be at home with her children, than to have all the modern-day luxuries, which are often called necessities. Many of these can be dispensed with in the interest of the development of the important mother-child relationships. There should be no better teacher than the mother. There should be no better home than where the children have the security of having their mother as the instructor in the important things of life. These include the developing of the spiritual values and character development, in an age where so many children grow up almost devoid of these most essential Christian values.

21

Prenuptial Agreements

THE term "prenuptial agreement" became increasingly common in the last part of the twentieth century. Very simply, a prenuptial agreement, while it can take many forms, is an agreement between a man and a woman contracted before they are married, usually detailing what the parties would receive should there be a breakup in the marriage in the years to come. Normally, in such an agreement the dominant issue is the distribution of resources: financial, properties, physical assets and how they will be divided at the time of a permanent separation or a divorce.

Prenuptial agreements are much more commonly forged by those who are wealthy. It is seen by some to be the way to avoid the normal practice of dividing the assets equally at the time of divorce. If legally binding, a prenuptial agreement supersedes the laws in many states. The laws of most states of America require the husband and wife receive 50% each of the assets, usually worked out in a legal, sometimes an acrimonious setting. Those opting for prenuptial agreement usually do so to secure personal assets. It is even more common among those where the marriage involves one partner being considerably wealthier than the other. It is more common also when the husband is much older than the wife.

Prenuptial agreements are more common in subsequent or second marriages. This is probably because late in life the assets at the time of the marriage are much more considerable than they would have been when the first marriage took place. In this age when significant numbers have multiple marriages, it becomes a greater factor because out of every divorce the one with the major assets would lose, substantially, the equity which had been built up over many years.

There is another reason for prenuptial agreements. Sometimes they address what will happen to any children who might be born to the marriage. This is a more difficult decision because it involves the lives of children long before the full issues which will lead to the divorce take place. It may be that the decision made will appear a very bad one in the light of subsequent events, and that such an agreement will lead to very unfortunate consequences for the children. We are not here simply dealing with assets or commodities. We are dealing with the lives of children who will be greatly affected by the divorce in so many other ways.

A third reason for prenuptial agreements occurs especially when an elderly person, usually a man, marries a younger woman. By the time the man marries, he has grown children and they are eyeing the assets which they would normally expect to inherit upon the death of their father, presumably well before the death of the younger woman he plans to marry. It is not surprising that a number of different emotions clash in such a situation. There is the natural avarice and greed of the children to participate in the distribution of the wealth of their father upon his death.

However, other considerations could well be the belief that the much younger woman is marrying their father, not for love, but rather for riches. Thus the children put great pressure upon their father to work out with them a prenuptial agreement. Typically, such an agreement will offer the wife, upon the death of their father, a very comfortable and expensive home, maybe a car and a certain lump sum financial payout.

We had a friend who, after the death of his first wife, became engaged to a younger woman. Though she was a fine Christian lady, because of the father's wealth, the children insisted on such an agreement, which fundamentally included the wife inheriting the very fine home in which they lived, receiving a settlement of a million dollars. We believe the settlement also included a car and household goods.

However, we return to the more common prenuptial agreement, which involves a financial agreement before marriage, involving no other people or considerations. Such an agreement is implicit evidence that there is no enduring commitment to the marriage vow. It implies that there is no certainty of the enduring love for the one he or she is marrying. It is almost a statement that sometime in the future, we will likely tire of each other or cast our affections in other directions. This is, surely, wholly inimical to marriage and its sacred, binding solemnity. It is not uncommon to place in such an agreement what the distribution of assets will be if the marriage lasts five years, as opposed to a better settlement if it lasts ten years.

Recently, as we prepare this volume, the issue of prenuptial agreement reached the headlines of some newspapers when two famous movie stars separated and divorced. It would seem that in their prenuptial agreement was a very favorable settlement to the spouse, should the marriage endure for ten years. However, the husband made the decision, not long before ten years, to dissolve the marriage. This is understandable, if there be any such deadlines. It stands to reason that great consideration will be given as to whether to continue with the marriage or to proceed with dissolution of the marriage. Such an agreement undoubtedly increases the likelihood that the marriage will not go the distance. While in this particular case we have little doubt that the spouse was not left destitute, yet it shows the secularization and fragility of marriage vows today. These vows are treated, not as "until death do us part" but as "until we lose interest in the other spouse," and probably set our eyes upon someone else. Such an attitude pays little regard for the heartache of such dissolutions, with often one spouse being deeply in love with the other, but that love not returned. Unrequited love is so cruel.

Generally speaking, prenuptial agreements represent an appalling state in society. Marriage is trivialized. These agreements recognize no enduring quality. They lead to a lack of caution in preparing for a marriage, and ultimately contribute to the moral collapse of society. This exacerbates the other aspects of society, at least in most western countries where the dissolution of marriage is a very simple process.

The introduction of no-fault divorces, the banality of adulterous affairs, the disregard for the anguished and devastated lives left after a divorce, is tragic. Selfishness, greed, avarice, and many other abominable sins form the foundation of these practices. Is it any wonder that young people today have such a perverted view of marriage, many considering it to be non-essential? Unless there be a moral revival of true Christianity, society will fall deeper into the abyss. One can only wonder what kind of vows such individuals make in their hearts at the time of their marriage.

22
Premarital Sexual Activity

FROM an early age, many, scarcely having reached their teenage years, are experimenting in sexual behavior. How tragic it is that immature youngsters are in circumstances which provide opportunities for such behavior. So often parents have little influence over their children and certainly few parameters, thus opening the door to a wide range of antisocial and immoral behavior. In the *Delta Democrat Times* in Greenville, Mississippi, October 26, 1988, Haven B. Gow, a radio and television commentator, as well as a news columnist, who has been published in more than one hundred magazines and newspapers, wrote an article entitled "Chastity Still a Wise Virtue." Gow presented the case for purity before marriage, summing it up this way:

> Essentially, the case for purity is based on respect; self-respect, respect for others, mutual respect; we cannot truly love others unless we respect their God-given, intrinsic moral worth and dignity.

In the article he quotes from high school teacher and college campus minister Robert Andrews' book, *The Family: God's Weapon for Victory,* Wine Press Publishing, Mukilteo, Washington, quoted in *Delta Democrat Times*, October 26, 1988.

Here are some statements from Andrews' book,

> Premarital sex causes a [woman] to lose respect for the man, but also to doubt that she, herself, is worthy of his esteem. . . . The loss of self-respect, and the feeling of worthlessness that follows, is a tremendous burden that is very difficult to unload. Lack of trust is another consequence of failing to remain sexually pure. Even when a man or woman eventually marries [his or her] sexual partner, there can be nagging questions as to that one's ability to remain faithful. . . .

> Finally, sexual impurity leads to lack of restraint. Countless women have yielded to the temptation to have sexual intercourse, fully believing that they would marry the man who was professing undying love for them. After the conquest was accomplished, the men were off to other pastures, eventually marrying women who would not yield to their sexual advances, and whom they, therefore, could "respect."   *Ibid.*

Gow also quoted another clergyman, James Toney, a Baptist scholar in Eudora, Arkansas.

> God, prayer and Bible reading were taken out of the public schools, and we now have drugs, crime, and the passing out of condoms and birth control pills instead. Unless we do a better job of teaching young people to believe in God and follow the Ten Commandments, we will find even more young people having premarital sex, illegitimate babies and abortions. *Ibid.*

Yet another Baptist pastor, John Redmond, Jr., of the Second Baptist Church, Lake Village, Arkansas, declared,

> We must uphold and teach the sacredness of sex, marriage, family and human life, even though it is unpopular today to do so; young people need to know the harmful physical, emotional, spiritual and moral consequences of prenuptial and irresponsible sexual activity. *Ibid.*

The quotation in the article is from Dr. Gary Smalley in his book, *Making Love Last Forever*, Word Publishing, Dallas. Dr. Smalley asserts that premarital sex and "living together" destroy the moral, spiritual and psychological foundation for a happy, successful and enduring marriage. He furnishes these reasons for rejecting premarital sex in favor of practicing chastity:

1. Premarital sex dulls our souls towards God and God's teachings and ways.
2. It reinforces selfishness and our sensual focus and keeps us from emphasizing love for God and others.
3. It hinders our awareness of the needs and feelings of others, especially our future spouses or good friends.
4. It leaves us vulnerable to sexual disease.
5. It increases our need for greater sexual stimulation, thereby increasing the potential for sensual conflict in marriage.
6. It leads to greater possibility of marriage discord and divorce.
7. It increases the possibility of sexual addiction.
8. It increases the possibility of guilt.
9. It leads to resentment and the feeling of being used and abused.
10. It can lead to unwanted pregnancy.
11. It can lead to abortions.

Gow further comments,

> Recent studies buttress the contention that premarital sex and "living together," undermine the psychological, moral and spiritual foundation of happy, successful and enduring marriages. *op. cit.*

He quotes a study by sociologists Larry Bumpass, James Sweet and Andrew Cherline. They found that

cohabitating unions are much less stable than unions that we gain as marriages.

Ibid.

He further stated that

40 percent of cohabitating unions break up before marriage and marriages that begin as cohabitating unions disrupt at a fifty percent higher rate than those that did not.

Ibid.

Gow quotes a 1991 study in Wisconsin conducted by Elizabeth Thomson and Ugo Collela, both social scientists, who found that thirteen thousand adults surveyed who had cohabitated before marriage reported

greater marital conflict and poorer communications than married couples who never had cohabitated before marriage.

Ibid.

Well we remember as children and youth growing up, that even respectable secular society, including those who had little religious interest, nevertheless held high moral values. However, the decline towards the permissiveness of today had its roots long before our childhood in what is called the "existentialist movement" of the nineteenth century, led by the Danish philosopher Søren Kierkegaard. Existentialism simply is "a philosophy centered upon the analysis of existence and stressing the freedom, responsibility, and usually the isolation of the individual" (*Merriam Webster Advanced Dictionary and Thesaurus*). Kierkegaard proclaimed that each one held his own standards of moral value. This concept denies that morality has absolutes which are derived from God and are enshrined in Holy Scriptures.

In the nineteenth century, almost the whole of Western society held to the moral integrity enunciated in the Bible and the law of God. Under such circumstances immorality, though practiced by some, was regarded by almost all members of society with great consternation. Any youth who fell into immorality brought disgrace and shame upon his or her family. With such clear standards of morality sustained by the majority of society, most young men and women went to the altar pure. However, with the breakdown of the moral leadership in the Christian churches, and with the increasing acceptance of the liberal agenda, and with the questioning of the infallibility of the Word of God, young people are left with little guidance. These ministers began to teach their congregations hedonistic principles and pandered to the materialistic motives of twentieth century parishioners. Increasingly, men and women disassociated themselves from the study of the Bible, and thus from the practice of its principles.

Society was cast into the dangerous quagmire of social mores rather than the pure streams of the divine principles of the Bible. Even then, the morality of society held high standards for a few more decades. In reality the social mores, whether acknowledged or not, followed the Bible principle of chastity and the high value of purity. Virginity was greatly honored and admired. Yet only briefly can social mores be maintained independent of the principles of Scripture, because mores are not established upon absolutes and therefore are highly susceptible to libertarian influences, exclusive of the foundation of the societal good. Children and youth soon become the victims of a society stripped of its protective parameters. Girls and woman have been greatly victimized as the baseness of carnal human nature has given free reign to vile lustful desires and practices.

By the latter part of the twentieth century there was a dramatic change— the existentialist concepts demanded the exercising of the rights of the individual to their own values and standards. The concept, that it is all right to do anything as long as you feel comfortable with it, soon emerged. What a tragic deception this is! It soon became common to hear crude statements such as "You must try it before you buy it," referring to premarital sex as the basis for marital preparation. As young men, we knew the fallacy of this kind of philosophy and were wise enough not to follow such folly. If a young man or young woman engaged in premarital sex, even if they subsequently married, the evidence to date points to the fact that the marriage is not likely to be as stable and happy as a home established by a marriage between responsible virgins.

Young people, let us keep in mind that God's Word is not simply counsel to be taken or rejected. It is a perfect pattern for human happiness and for a fulfilling life. The self control exercised by young men and women before marriage is a wonderful precursor to a happy and successful marriage. Well Colin remembers an experience he had as speaker at a camp meeting in Indiana. At the camp he delivered nineteen presentations, mostly to the youth and young people. The whole series of meetings was directed toward the surrender of the young peoples' lives to the Lord, and much time was given to the principles of purity and chastity, before marriage and in the marriage relationship.

The invitation for him to speak was initiated by a pastor who had heard Colin preach on some of these issues and was greatly attracted to the message. However, as Colin was later to discover, there was considerable anger among some of the young pastors who listened to his first presentation. They were reported to have made comments such as, "The young people will never put up with this. This man comes on too strongly." These pastors were completely silenced by the end of the series of presentations, when about double the number of young people were present to hear those later messages. As a side issue, we would urge pastors and teachers to be frank, open and very clear on these issues. Truly the young people desire to know the best principles; those which originate with God.

Two young ladies about to start their senior year in academy approached Colin the night he preached on the topic "Going to the Altar Pure." These two attractive young ladies explained that many of their peers had broken down and were involved or had been involved in sexual activity. They both wondered if there were something wrong with them. They said to Colin, "We were about to break down ourselves." How rewarded Colin was when their last words were "Tonight we made a commitment to go to the altar pure." I pray that those two precious young ladies today have wonderful marriages. Christian marriages, built upon Biblical morality which leads to purity throughout life, are the most enduring. We also hope that they followed the counsel from other presentations concerning the choice of a life partner so that they married men of the same integrity which they had determined to uphold.

Our goal in writing this book is to help every reader to be part of an army of youth who will reverse the tragic libertarian trends where so many young people do that which comes naturally. Remember, the Bible says,

> The heart is deceitful above all things, and desperately wicked: who can know it.   Jeremiah 17:9

Remember also that the only way you can follow the pathway of Christian morality is by daily surrender of your will to the power of the indwelling Savior.

23

Abortion

WHEN Russell was a medical student training at the University of Sydney in Australia, all the students were solemnly warned against performing any form of permissive abortion. It was pointed out that doctors guilty of this crime were sentenced normally to between five and seven years in prison; they lost their medical license and their disqualification to practice medicine was shared to many countries of the world. Effectively, even after they were released from prison, their medical practice was over.

What a different age we are in today. In the United States, since the enactment of the *Roe vs. Wade* Supreme Court decision, the floodgate has opened to permissive abortion, and it is estimated that about one and one half million prenates are legally aborted in the United States every year. The numbers around the world must be horrendous. Many justify abortion by pointing to the fact that the planet is already overpopulated with human beings, and that this has a devastating effect upon the planet's ecology. Others have vigorously defended abortion on the right of the mother to choose. We cannot support such shallow reasoning. If, irresponsibly, a babe is initiated, it is society's obligation to protect this weakest of the weak from being murdered.

We were born in 1933, the same year that the Nazi Party of Adolf Hitler gained government in Germany. As little lads we were horrorstruck by reports that Hitler had ordered the murder of every defective child born. In view of the society of the era of the nineteen thirties and nineteen forties, this decree certified Hitler's credentials as a vile monster. In History classes in primary school, we were equally appalled to learn that the Spartans of Greece destroyed all handicapped babies born by casting them, in winter, into the snow.

Such crimes undoubtedly denote a godless society, all the excuses proffered notwithstanding. Yet today we deprive of life not only handicapped children, but also perfectly normal children. We can only conclude that modern society is worse than the German society under Adolf Hitler and the ancient Spartan society on this issue.

At the end of 2003, Russell and all our family went through the agonizing crisis of his son and daughter-in-law. They were expecting their first child but late complications developed which threatened the life of the mother and also, obviously, the little babe in the womb. The hospital exerted heroic efforts to save the life of both mother and child and this they did with wonderful success. However, the little one was born nine weeks prematurely, weighing two pounds, thirteen ounces. For seven weeks Shea remained in hospital in the Intensive Care Unit (ICU) until she was strong enough to return home with her mother and father. Even then, for many more weeks, there were visits in the home by pediatric nurses to monitor the progress of little Shea. Today she is a healthy, wonderful little girl. Yet it seems so ironic that such heroic efforts were made, when many other fetuses are killed, some even more advanced than little Shea was.

Let us examine the reasons why there are so many unwanted pregnancies. Number one, of course, is the promiscuity of this age in which many irresponsible adults strongly teach and urge, not chastity, not morality, but ways in which to avoid the consequences of premarital or extramarital sex, all in the name of *compassion*.

As we have had to deal with these situations, Russell, as a physician, had to make decisions himself when young women would come to him seeking an abortion. He resolutely refused to conduct a permissive abortion in his long years as a physician. He made every effort to encourage such young ladies not to go ahead with an abortion. In compassion he spoke to those seeking abortion, explaining the wonderful options which they had to carry the child to full pregnancy and then, if unable or unwilling to care for the newborn, to place the baby for adoption in the home of caring parents to bring the child up and give it the opportunity of life. Of course the young lady still has a decision to make. Yet he did the best he could to counsel each one to follow moral principles of the sanctity of life. Colin, as a trained psychologist and educator, also has sought to encourage young women against going ahead with an abortion.

Second, abortion reflects the fact that all the education in the world will not stop unwanted pregnancy. Young people can be encouraged in birth control, they can be assured of the effectiveness of the "night after" pills, but the reality is that because of their lack of Christian conversion, their immaturity and inexperience, many young people will be confronted with the reality that a new life has been initiated into the world. So often it is a result of an uncontrolled lifestyle which results in a pregnancy. Frequently it is the result of the unrestrained passions of young people who have plunged into immorality.

Today the teaching of chastity, the virtue of virginity before marriage, and uncompromising morality are considered by many in society to be unreasonable. We have heard statements along these lines, "It is no use telling the young people not to engage in sexual activity. Therefore our efforts should be directed to educate them to engage only in protected sex." We reject categorically, out of hand, such an assertion. Properly educated and carefully directed by their parents, young people can be trained to eschew the evil of fornication. The facts of history attest to that. Thorough training in Biblical principles and the protecting power of Christ are able to sustain the purity of youth and young people and protect them from a life of heartache and tragic sexually transmitted diseases..

We can never forget one of our fellow college friends. Many years later this godly man was the father of two teen-aged daughters. At the appropriate time he sat his daughters down and explained to them, "You may not be happy with some of the parameters which Dad will place upon you. You may be resistant to some of the times when your Father will not permit you to go or do what you are planning to do. But Father is determined to get you to the altar pure." We remember well when years later the father could speak of his success. "Both daughters are married now" and with great joy in his heart he said, "Both went to the altar pure."

There is great decadence in today's society, society which the Bible describes "As it was in the days of Noe" (Luke 17:26) and "in the days of Lot" (Luke 17:28). Warped thinking has developed among irresponsible adults who are prepared to ever encourage, or at least not discourage, their children to live a life of promiscuity. Indeed, this thinking has greatly invaded into the portals of Christianity ; and many professed Christians, pastors and others in ecclesiastical authority, believe they are showing compassion and understanding when they counsel young people to practice protected sex. We have learned that in the military many chaplains routinely give this counsel to young soldiers. How misguided such individuals are. They are bringing a pall of grief upon the young people to whom they offer such warped counsel and, perhaps of least importance is the fact that there is no such thing as complete certainty of the effectiveness of so-called protected sex.

When Russell was practicing in a Mission Hospital in Penang, Malaysia, during the Vietnam War, he treated a large number of American servicemen who had come to Penang for "R and R" (rest and recuperation). Routinely they were provided a hotel room and a prostitute by the military authorities. Many contracted gonorrhea and/or syphilis. The naval lieutenant-commander who was the officer in charge of this project used to joke about bringing "another one" for Russell's medical care.

One day, a very serious lieutenant commander, his expression revealing embarrassment, entered Russell's consulting room. None of his former light-heartedness over the plight of other servicemen was evident, for he, too, had fallen a victim to venereal disease. He was panic stricken, for his wife was due to visit him from the United States in two weeks time. He pled with Russell to do everything he could to hasten his recovery, claiming, unconvincingly, that he had been lured from his period of chastity by one of the prostitutes who desired sexual relations from the commanding officer!

Second, even if the initiation of a babe does not take place, the protection against sexually transmitted disease can fail, and sexual participants are liable to be infected with one or more of these diseases, some of which can be fatal. We cannot but weep over the millions who are facing certain death because of promiscuity. Biblical morality is the only true safeguard for young people. Certainly, even if permissive sexual behavior does not result in conception, or the experiencing of a sexually transmitted disease, there are other consequences which can reap lifelong damage to a person. The guilt, the shame, the remorse, the self-condemnation which is so often experienced, especially by young ladies, leave lifetime scars. In his many years as an educator, Colin has had the experience of attempting to help such emotionally damaged young ladies. Premarital sex will often spoil forever the beauty of the sanctity of loving sex in the marriage relationship. It can bring tremendous tensions into the marriage, and even be a precursor of divorce.

Let us share with you some examples. A young lady was seduced by her suitor, who claimed to be a Christian. Indeed, the young man was the son of a pastor. Eventually she wavered and surrendered to his seductive pressure. A new life was initiated. She told the young man the situation. He was horrified and urged her to seek an abortion quickly. She was deeply convicted not to do so. Eventually, however, the pressure of the young man caused her to add another sin to the first sin. She aborted the child.

Colin first met this young lady six years after the abortion had taken place. However, she could not forget how old that little child would have been had it not been aborted. Every time she saw a child about the age her little one would have been, she would break into tears. By the way, the young man soon discarded her and when Colin met her she was still a single lady filled with remorse, emotional instability and guilt. Compassionately, Colin sought to raise before her the forgiving power of the gospel, the loving wooing of Jesus and His great promise,

> If we confess our sins, he is faithful and just to forgive us our sins, and to cleanse us from all unrighteousness.   1 John 1:9

Yet unquestionably, the emotional scars were deep. Whether she was able ever to enter into a successful marriage, he does not know.

When Colin was chairman of the Psychology Department of a Christian college, one day his office door burst open without a knock. Here was a young woman in her late twenties who sobbed uncontrollably and fell down at Colin's knees. This was a very difficult situation for him. He had no idea of the cause of the sobbing. He did not know the young lady very well for she was not a psychology major but a nursing major. It took some minutes before this distraught woman was able, through her sobs, to explain the cause of her emotional upheaval. She had just attended a class in prenatal anatomy and physiology addressing the development of embryo and fetus and the early development of the neonate and infant. Guilt overwhelmed her because nine and seven years before, she had had abortions. She could not forgive herself. She was emotionally torn with what she had done. Colin again did everything to explain the mercy, the love and forgiveness of Jesus. Though she was attending this Christian college, she herself was not a Christian. She had no hope and no understanding of the love of God and His forgiveness. Colin could only hope that she later may have found the beauty of the gospel of Jesus. He hoped that she was not damaged irreparably for the rest of her life. How burdened Colin was for her. Because she was without any orientation to Christianity, there was nothing he could do to help alleviate her terrible distress.

When Russell was Director of the Enton Hall Health Centre, near Godalming in Surrey, England in the early 1980s, he treated an eighty-year-old German Jewish former refugee. A married woman in her early thirties, she had fallen pregnant. However when Hitler gained political power in Germany, she recognized that there would be a bleak future for Jewish children in Germany. She was not a practicing religious Jewess and thus sought an abortion.

Half a century later she was still tormented by the decision she had taken. No day passed without the anguish of her decision rending her peace of mind. As she possessed no faith in Christ or the Father and their tender loving forgiveness for the repentant, Russell was at an utter loss to bring the only source of peace and comfort to her breast.

Many have agreed that in normal circumstances they oppose abortion. However, some of these argue that in this day of medical science where it can be determined whether or not the child is physically normal well before birth, that in some cases it would be better for the fetus to be aborted. Who are we to play God? We know some situations which are shocking. For example, Colin recalls a man he met who was born mentally retarded, blind and deaf. This man was probably around forty years of age when Colin first saw him. The man had so little communication, yet the family which was caring for him did so with such tender love that they were able to transmit that love to him. He had been taught to feed himself and even to help dress himself. When the surrogate mother would put her cheek to his cheek and show loving compassion to him, there was a very wonderful response.

Years ago *Readers Digest* carried a story that long has remained in our minds. It was the story of a mother and her son. When she was pregnant she learned that the child would be physically deformed. The doctor urged her to abort, but the mother, a dedicated Christian, refused. The child was seriously deformed without legs and with stubby feet. But the love of his mother never wavered and she did everything possible to bring him up with as normal a life as possible. There was no dysfunction in his upper body and she had him trained as a violinist. At the time of the article this young man had become a brilliant violinist greatly acclaimed on concert tours. We cannot play God. What a joy this young man was to his mother.

Some others have argued that they cannot oppose abortion in some of the most desperate situations, especially children who are conceived as result of rape. While this is not overly common, it certainly does happen. Colin has met two such mothers. The first mother he met when her child was eighteen years of age. What a fine young man he was. As a college student she had been unconverted and had deceptively left her dormitory on a number of occasions and had been taken by men to bars. On this occasion, apparently her escort placed some drug into her drink and she passed out and clearly the sexual act took place while she was unconscious, a despicable case of rape. However, this woman, though at the time not practicing the life of a Christian, still made the moral decision not to abort. You can only imagine what joy she has that her son grew up to be a dedicated Christian and was very deeply involved in the spiritual life of his church.

Another case came to the attention of Colin. He was staying in the home of one of the members of the church where he was preaching. Also in the home was a West Indian mother and her five-month-old daughter. It was obvious how much the mother loved that daughter, and yet Colin learned at the home where she was staying that the babe was the result of incestuous rape involving one of her own family members. Of course such an act could be very dangerous. The related genetic pool could lead to the great possibility of physical or mental defects. However, this woman too refused to abort, and it was obvious that by God's grace, this little infant was normal in every way, alert and very much consistent with the patterns of a five-month-old baby.

God is calling us to take the high ground. Even in the issue of rape we do not have the right to kill an embryo or a fetus. Of course, we pray that none of these occurrences have taken place in the life of the readers. However, again we emphasize that if a reader has been involved in premarital sex, or has been involved in an abortion, we uphold to you the loving God who is "not willing that any should perish, but that all should come to repentance" (2 Peter 3:9), the One who has promised His unfailing forgiveness to all who confess and repent of their sins. He will take away the guilt, He will take away the condemnation, as you resolve never again to violate these principles of chastity and morality. People in all ages have had to swim against the current of worldly opinion and practices. Today the current is much stronger than it has been in past history. Yet godly young people will never be conformers, but they will be transformed.

> And be not conformed to this world: but be ye transformed by the renewing of your mind, that ye may prove what is that good, and acceptable, and perfect, will of God. Romans 12:2

24

Alternative Lifestyles

TODAY some countries' legislative bodies have outlawed any statement which reflects negatively upon what are euphemistically and commonly called alternative lifestyles. By this they mean those lifestyles which are forbidden in the sacred Word of God. Those practicing homosexual and lesbian lifestyles with emblazoned boldness have "gay-pride week." Others are called Mardi Gras which are "celebrations" of so-called gay liberation. Many cities have vulgar parades as, for example in Sydney, the largest city in our own homeland of Australia. The annual gay and lesbian parade through Sydney is the largest such parade in the world and is nationally televised. This is called progress, human rights, equality. We are not here addressing the issue of equal rights in the work place. We are addressing the fact that there are many who are urged to "come out of the closet" and make known their immoral practices which, like all immorality, are forbidden in the sacred Word of God. Even gay policemen march in this parade.

Educational curricula in many nations of the world are designed, not to educate youth in the noble principles of God's protective parameters, but encourage young people to believe that base immorality is equally acceptable with the expression of true love in a monogamous sexual relationship between a married man and woman. Many church leaders teach the same. Army chaplains now encourage "responsible sex" by handing out condoms. Surely we are in the days of Sodom and Gomorrah.

After speaking against the homosexual lifestyle and practices during a week of prayer at a boarding academy, Colin was approached by about a dozen male students seeking further explanations. He pointed out that he had made the situation very plain by reading a number of texts from the Scripture which settled the issue of the practice of homosexuality beyond any doubt. Still some of the students pressed him and so again Colin made it plain that homosexual and lesbian practices were an abomination to God. Some of the students were startled. Then, after a pause, a number of the youth turned to one of the boys in the group and said, "Didn't we tell you so?" In one sense Colin felt embarrassed for that youth because obviously he was engaged in such activities. However Colin did not stop there, for he assured the youth of the wonderful love and power of the Savior to provide the strength to live victoriously.

The Scriptures, both Old and New Testaments, warn against homosexual practices.

Thou shalt not lie with mankind, as with womankind: it is abomination.
Leviticus 18:22

If a man also lie with mankind, as he lieth with a woman, both of them have committed an abomination: they shall surely be put to death; their blood shall be upon them.
Leviticus 20:13

Without understanding, covenant breakers, without natural affection [homosexuality], implacable, unmerciful: Who, knowing the judgment of God, that they which commit such things are worthy of death, not only do the same, but have pleasure in them that do them.
Romans 1:31,–32

Know ye not that the unrighteous shall not inherit the kingdom of God? Be not deceived: neither fornicators, nor idolaters, nor adulterers, nor effeminate, nor abusers of themselves with mankind.
1 Corinthians 6:9

And likewise also the men, leaving the natural use of the woman, burned in their lust one toward another; men with men working that which is unseemly, and receiving in themselves that recompense of their error which was meet.
Romans 1:27

For whoremongers, for them that defile themselves with mankind, for menstealers, for liars, for perjured persons, and if there be any other thing that is contrary to sound doctrine.
1 Timothy 1:10

While there are not so many texts against lesbianism, it too is addressed with similar warnings.

For this cause God gave them up unto vile affections: for even their women did change the natural use into that which is against nature.
Romans 1:26

Now young people, these texts are very plain. The passage of time or the changing mores of society have not altered the infallible words of God. There are many claims today that society is totally different and that there have always been homosexually oriented individuals. No doubt this is true. However, we dispute the claims that there seem to be many more practicing homosexuals today than in former generations only because the homosexuals have "come out of the closet." Today's society encourages this practice. There has been a tremendous acceleration of the homosexual lifestyle, in large part because Hollywood has openly and brazenly promoted it. The breakdown of home life and marriages has greatly contributed to this lifestyle. It is well attested in creditable research that those who have no father or who have had abusive fathers are more likely to engage in the homosexual lifestyle than those who come from stable homes where the role differentiation between mother and father is very plain. Young ladies who become disaffected from their mothers and closer to their fathers are more likely to enter the lesbian lifestyle.

Corruption and degradation in society are adding greatly to the number of those who participate in such a lifestyle. The determination of the gay activists became very obvious to Colin when he was president of a Christian college in Maryland. He was approached by a student who asked him a simple question, "Can God continue to bless this institution when we have a practicing homosexual student on our campus?" Colin asked him for further explanation. He said that one of the students was then practicing this lifestyle. He asked him if he loved the college sufficiently to identify this young man and to share his concerns with the Chairman of the Citizenship Committee. He said he was willing to do so in the presence of the young man, and this took place.

The accused student, to his credit, confirmed the truth of the allegations. However he resorted to the defense that he was not a dormitory student and therefore did not come under the rules of the institution in this respect. As president of the college, Colin had an entirely different understanding of the college's responsibility. When the young man was asked if he would counsel with a Christian counselor on the faculty, he agreed to do so, but attended only once, deciding it was not worthwhile to talk with the counselor because he had "old-fashioned concepts of homosexuality." When the chairman of the Citizenship Committee asked what he should do, Colin told him that the members of the Committee had no alternative but to take disciplinary action against the student so that the Institution could uphold the integrity of the principles upon which the college had been established. The chairman asked if Colin would attend the meeting. He agreed, even though it was not his normal practice. The committee met with the young man—a fine-looking and talented specimen of manhood. Colin made one last plea to him. The only response he received was "You are one way and I am the other." The committee had no valid alternative but, in great sadness, to ask him to withdraw from the college.

During the next chapel exercise for the staff and students, a faculty member came to the platform to whisper to Colin that there were many gay-activists outside the church picketing the institution. The faculty member asked Colin, "Should we call the police?" Colin asked, "Where are they located?" "On the sidewalk." "The police can take no action, for that is public property," Colin responded, "All we can do is to pray." When the chapel dismissed, Colin observed eighteen men and one woman holding up placards declaring among other things, "Rise up against this oppressive administration." "Ten percent of the students and faculty here are gay. Stand shoulder to shoulder against this decision." Understand that this was a very difficult situation for Colin. He did not know what would be the reaction on the campus. However, by the grace of God, he found that negative attitudes to the College decision were very few indeed. It was limited to five young ladies who asked how fair it was to send away a young man without providing help for him first. Patiently Colin explained the efforts which had been made and the rejection of those efforts.

This was only the beginning of the opposition. Later Colin received a telephone call from a Gay Rights lawyer practicing in Baltimore, asking to visit Colin's office to dialogue a financial settlement for the damage inflicted upon this young man's reputation by the college. Colin requested a Christian lawyer to sit with him in the interview. Not only did this gay-activist lawyer arrive, but also the President of the Gay Activist Movement of Washington, D. C. attended with the expelled student. While the lawyer proved to be a gracious man, the gentleman from the Gay Activist Movement proved to be very aggressive. He continued to insist that Colin agree to discuss an out-of-court settlement. Colin simply asked him, "What damage has the college done to this young man's reputation? It was the Gay Activists themselves who proclaimed the homosexual orientation of this young man. In any case," Colin asked, "surely you would not believe that to call a young man a homosexual was damaging to his reputation?"

Colin also asked, "Why did you declare that ten percent of our faculty and students were 'gay'?" His response was, "Ten percent of any population." Colin said, "Maybe so in the population at large, but it is certainly not so on this campus." The gay activist lawyer claimed discrimination in that the college had not acted in the same way to students engaged in heterosexual sex. Colin was able to respond that the very summer before this had taken place, the college had expelled a young man and young woman for fornication. The college had dealt with the heterosexual fornication situation in the same way it responded to the homosexual student. The lawyer supporting Colin made only one comment, "My client does not desire to go to court. But if it means going to court to uphold the moral standards of this institution, he is ready to go." Colin's lawyer friend was accurate in what he had said. It became plain that they realized that they did not have a case.

However, shortly afterward Colin received a call from a reporter from the major newspaper serving the region . "A former student from your college who has been expelled has given us a long statement alleging mal-practice by the college. I want to give you the opportunity to present your side of the story." Colin told the reporter that he was unwilling to comment on specifics of the case. However he was willing to provide a statement on the college's position concerning homosexuality, which he did.

Numbers of times the reporter attempted to draw Colin into a more specific statement concerning the individual, but Colin stood firm. Eventually the reporter contacted the Chairman of the Citizenship Committee who gave a specific statement to the reporter. Unbeknown to Colin, a newspaper reporter and photographer came to the campus, took photographs, interviewed students and the Vice-President of the Student Association of the college, having not been able to contact the Student Association President. The article occupied three-quarters of a page in the newspaper, declaring that the homosexual issue had come back to the region again. However the paper treated the college very well. It said that they had found no real support for the dismissed student on campus among the students, and that the Vice-President of the Student Association had said that while he was sad to see the student leave, nevertheless he felt that the college had no other alternative in the circumstances.

Even this was not the end of the situation, for members of a gay activist group came to the college's radio station asking for equal time to present their views concerning homosexual issues on the college radio station. At that time the FCC required equal time for opposing views to be presented on matters involving issues of public interest. The radio manager came over to Colin very alarmed. "What will I do?" Colin responded, "What has been broadcast on our radio station on the issue of homosexuality?" He said that there had been no direct programs but sometimes the issue of homosexuality had come up in talk-back programs. Colin told the radio manager that even if the college radio station was closed down, he refused to have any time given to pro-homosexual presentations on the radio. In any case, Colin told him that these people would have to find what had been said that they are claiming was damaging to the homosexual cause. That never happened. At last the harassment ended.

Christians cannot compromise on this situation. However, the authors are very compassionate with those who may be tempted in this area. Both of us have sought earnestly to help young people in this situation. Indeed, in some cases we believe we have been successful. We offer some counsel. Colin was talking with a young lady in Sweden who asked if he could help her with a dilemma which she had. She was in correspondence with a young man who had confided to her that he was a practicing homosexual but also a Christian. She had attempted to counsel him but he had responded by e-mail that for eight years he had prayed for God to take away the temptation of homosexuality, but God had chosen not to do so; so he believed that therefore God did not condemn him for this ongoing practice. Colin's response to the young lady was, "This young man is praying the wrong prayer. If we could simply gain victory by asking God to remove all temptation from us, then there would not be the powerful spiritual growth that all of us must have in our preparation for heaven. Jesus Himself went through the fiercest temptations. Temptation is not sin. God does not take away temptation. However, God has, through Christ, provided the power to overcome temptation.

> There hath no temptation taken you but such as is common to man: but God is faithful, who will not suffer you to be tempted above that ye are able; but will with the temptation also make a way to escape, that ye may be able to bear it.
>
> 1 Corinthians 10:13

> Submit yourselves therefore to God. Resist the devil, and he will flee from you.
>
> James 4:7

Colin's counsel to the young lady was to tell this young man that his prayer must be for divine power every day as he submits his life to Jesus to overcome the temptation. He also suggested that he be counseled to do everything to avoid circumstances which might intensify temptation, so that he might live a life of purity in the sight of his heavenly Maker. This is surely wise counsel to all who face temptation in the area of homosexual and lesbian relationships, or in any other area of sin.

25

Same-sex Marriages

IT is reported that during the nineteenth century Queen Victoria of Great Britain received a bill to be signed into law, which had been passed by the House of Commons and House of Lords, outlawing homosexual and lesbian relationships. She resolutely refused to sign the bill into law on the basis that she adamantly believed that there were no same-sex relationships between women. Ultimately, the law was signed, but only outlawing sex between two males. If this story be true, it demonstrated a high level of naiveté on the part of the Queen, who was held in high esteem. Unquestionably, same-sex relationships between women have a long profile down through the history of the world.

There is no doubt that women living together create much less comment or suspicion than two men cohabiting in the same dwelling. However, the practice of lesbianism, like homosexuality, dates back to antiquity. The question of same-sex marriage has become a topic of intense debate in modern times. In recent history in the western world, the homosexual lobby has been an extraordinarily active and successful one. It has been able to convince the majority of their rights and legitimacy.

While in this book we are not addressing all the various rights which the homosexual lobby has succeeded in achieving, we will address the issue of homosexual marriages. In some regions of the world, it is considered a hate crime to question the right of homosexuals to marry, but no Bible-believing Christian can be silent, because the eternal life of these practicing homosexuals is at stake. We repeat here the warnings from Scripture.

> Without understanding, covenant breakers, without natural affection [homosexuality], implacable, unmerciful: who knowing the judgment of God, that they which commit such things are worthy of death, not only do the same, but have pleasure in them that do them. Romans 1:31–32

> If a man also lie with mankind, as he lieth with a woman, both of them have committed an abomination: they shall surely be put to death; their blood shall be upon them. Leviticus 20:13

Thou shalt not lie with mankind, as with womankind: it is abomination.

Leviticus 18:22

Know ye not that the unrighteous shall not inherit the kingdom of God? Be not deceived: neither fornicators, nor idolaters, nor adulterers, nor effeminate, nor abusers of themselves with mankind. I Corinthians 6:9

[26] For this cause God gave them up unto vile affections: for even their women did change the natural use into that which is against nature; [27] And likewise also the men, leaving the natural use of the woman, burned in their lust one toward another; men with men working that which is unseemly, and receiving in themselves that recompense of their error which was meet. Romans 1:26–27

For whoremongers, for them that defile themselves with mankind, for menstealers, for liars, for perjured persons, and if there by any other thing that is contrary to sound doctrine. 1 Timothy 1:10

The issues are quite plain. For example, in the first chapter of Romans, verse 26, women are said to have changed their natural use into that which is against nature. In verse 27, there is the same condemnation against men in the practice of homosexuality. These are placed in a very long list of sins which God condemns including maliciousness, murder, deceit, hatred. In verse 32, Paul explains that those involved in any of these practices of sin will face a judgment in which they will be found guilty and worthy of eternal death. All Bible-believing Christians have no alternative other than to explain God's plain condemnation of same-sex practices. All Christians have the responsibility to explain the loving power of God to provide grace and strength to gain victory over all sin including homosexuality and lesbianism.

This certainly is not a popular message today. There is much opposition mounted against those who, in Christian love and concern, raise these issues. We have great compassion for those who are tempted in this area. Sins of a sexual nature are a great challenge, for victory over these sins is not easy, but God is an all powerful God. Surely He has the power to give to us the victory, not only over those sins which we have adopted during the experiences of life, but also those biological tendencies which we may have inherited. There is no question that down through history some of the most difficult sins to overcome have been sins of our carnal nature. However there are those who, through the power of the indwelling Jesus, have overcome these passions.

Even among homosexual and lesbian partners there is evidence that God has placed within the heart of humans the need for men and women to complement each other in the marriage relationships. Almost inevitably in homosexual and lesbian liaisons, one partner is clearly playing the male role and the other the female role. This is often accentuated in the way each partner dresses.

As a lifelong educator, Colin has been able to help a number of young men who have been beleaguered with homosexual temptation. It has not been easy for anyone. He recalls the situation of a young man who attended a Christian college in Australia, when Colin was Chairman of the Education Department. Like himself, this young man was an identical twin. He told of his suspicions that he had homosexual attractions which he had attempted to deny for a long time. One day, when doing missionary work for the Lord, he had come to the home of a man who apparently was a practicing homosexual. This man perceived something about this Christian youth which caused him to identify him as homosexual too. Now, this young man was not practicing homosexuality. Yet it was this situation which led him to seek counsel and support from Colin. He explained that he had much stronger affectionate feelings for other young men than he did for young women. Colin advised him that every day he should earnestly place this temptation before the Lord, asking for the power of victory one day at a time. Colin further encouraged him not to consider marriage unless he had first gained a day-by-day victory over these temptations. He promised Colin that he would not do so, for lacking in victory can cause much heartache in a marriage.

After Colin left Australia to serve in Jamaica, he learned that the young man had married. Colin prayed that was the signal that he had gained victory. Sad though it may seem, some may even have to take the step of not marrying at all. They can use their time and energies effectively in the service of the King of kings and Lord of lords, and God will bless them, and constantly they will receive the strength of Jesus, if every day they are submitted to Him.

Submit yourselves therefore to God. Resist the devil, and he will flee from you.
James 4:7

God does not take every temptation away from us. Sometimes we have to battle for years; maybe it can become a lifetime battle against some temptations. Our earnest prayer must be for God to provide the fullness of His power to meet the temptation. There is one certain consequence of this. Every day we win the victory this weakens the temptation, but that does not call for lowering our vigilance, for Satan waits eagerly for moments when we are off guard. However, the Bible promises are sure:

Now unto him that is able to keep you from falling, and to present you faultless before the presence of his glory with exceeding joy.   Jude 24

For I am not ashamed of the gospel of Christ: for it is the power of God unto salvation to every one that believeth: to the Jew first, and also to the Greek.

Romans 1:16

There are thoughts to which we must not yield—first, that God cannot give us the victory; second, that we are too weak to gain the victory; third, that we can gain heaven while continuing in the practice of sin. That includes homosexuality. For those who feel beleaguered by this terrible temptation, we would recommend the book by Victor J. Adamson, *That Kind Can Never Change! Can They?*, 2000, Huntington House Publishers, or accessed on the website: www.victoradamson.com.

We pray for victory for all those ensnared in homosexual practices. God has the power. Make sure you make complete submission of your life to Him, moment by moment.

26

Divorce in Australia

AN article in the *Australian Woman's Weekly* entitled "We've Come A Long Way, Baby" revealed a dramatic change in lifestyle for Australian women over a period of seventy years. While the article was designed to look at the positive advances on behalf of women, nevertheless, the statistics revealed a much darker side. *Australian Woman's Weekly* magazine was first published June 8, 1933; therefore, it was comparing the statistics of 1933 with those of 2003, the year of the magazine's seventieth anniversary. It so happened that the authors of this book were born a few months after the first number of *Australian Woman's Weekly* was published.

There is no doubt that the magazine was taking credit for some of the dramatic improvement in conditions for women during the seventy years of its publication. No doubt the magazine contributed to the women's revolution. It is probably impossible to evaluate, but we do recognize one of the greatest contributions to the changes in the lifestyle of women has much to do with the culture of the media, especially since the advent of television.

However, we cannot underestimate, also, the dramatic changes that came as the result of World War II. In Australia, it was probably even more dramatic than in the United States of America. At the time, Australia's population was about seven million with a territory comparable to the land mass of the contiguous 48 states of the United States.

When Britain declared war on Nazi Germany in 1939, Australia followed a few hours later. Hundreds of thousands of young men were sent to fight on behalf of the motherland (Great Britain) in Europe and in North Africa. However, November 7, 1941, the whole Pacific area became engulfed in war as a result of the Japanese attack on Pearl Harbor. The work force of Australia was stretched far beyond its human resources.

Thus, for the first time in the history of this new nation, large numbers of ladies, including married women, were urged to join the work force. Many ladies served in the military, others on the land, often called land girls, working to help the farmers, many of whose sons had been drafted into the Australian military. Others worked in munitions factories. Still others worked in the wholesale and retail sectors of business. In 1942, the Women's Employment Board (formed to draft women into essential wartime work) offered higher rates of pay than had ever before been available to female workers. This greatly encouraged married women to join the work force. Further, many of the husbands of these workers had been rushed into the army, and many had been sent overseas. A significant percentage of these married women had not yet commenced a family. Therefore they smoothly fitted well into the work force. After the completion of the war, many of these married women who had enjoyed the higher standard of living afforded them by being a part of the labor force, decided to continue employment. Whereas before the war, working mothers were frowned upon, except when required by necessity, now they became well accepted.

Soon society adapted to the needs of these wives, many of whom were now mothers, by providing day-care centers, pre-school kindergartens and other social services. The *Woman's Weekly* article rightly stated, "In the seventy years since 1933, who could have possibly predicted how dramatically different life would become for Australian women and consequentially of the Australian family? Today we are better educated, more financially independent, living longer, and in charge of our futures—but are we happier?" (We've Come a Long Way, Baby, *Australian Woman's Weekly*, October 2003). The last four words pose a question which we believe many Australian women will be forced to answer in the negative.

This is the question which all young people would do well to ponder. Of course, it is very difficult to evaluate the happiness factor during the severe worldwide economic depression of the late 1920s and the 1930s and the happiness factor during the consumer-driven society of today. However, there are factors which can be evaluated.

Let us examine some of the statistics and data which were provided in this article which normally would be considered to be favorable statistics. In Australia, in 1933, 5% of women between the age of 25 and 54 were in the work force. In 2003, 61% were in the work force. In 1933, the average female weekly wage was 43 shillings and 5 pence. [approximately $4.34 per week] which was about 54% of the average male wage. In 2003, the average female weekly wage was $820, 84% of the average weekly male wage. In 1933 only 16% of females, age 16, were still at school. In 2003, 82% of female, age 16, were still at school. In 1933, infant mortality rate was 39.52 babies per 1,000 live births: in 2003 the rate was 4.8 per 1000. In 1933, the mortality rate of women during pregnancy and childbirth was

431 out of 25,867 deaths, nationally. In 2003, it was 12 out of 61,709 deaths, nationally. In 1933, a woman's life expectancy was 67.1 years. In 2003, the woman's life expectancy was 82.4 years. Add to that, women's average height is almost 3 centimeters, or 1 inch taller. Between the ages of 20 and 39, their average weight is almost 4.4 kilos, or approximately 10 pounds more. All the physical measurements have also commensurately increased.

The change in Australian society concerning women is very educative. In 1933, there were no female Parliamentarians. In 2003, 27% of Parliamentarians were women, with the first woman elected to the lower house, the House of Representatives, in 1943. In 1949, the first woman to become a Cabinet member of government was appointed. In 1950, the wage laws were changed so that the basic wage (minimum wage) for women was set at 75% of the male basic wage. It took until 1969 for the Australian Conciliation and Arbitration Commission to rule that "Equal pay for equal work was to be phased in by 1972."

Women have also made great gains in the legal field. In 1962, the first woman was elevated to become a Queen's Counsel, the title given to barristers (trial lawyers) who have achieved great eminence. Consequently, women have become cabinet ministers and leaders of political parties. In 1987, a woman was elevated as a justice of the seven-member High Court of Australia, Australia's highest court. Females have been elected Chief Minister of the Australian Capital Territory and Premiers of State Parliaments (Western Australia and Victoria), as well as a governor of a State (New South Wales) (*Ibid.*).

However, let us come back to the question raised in the article. "Today, we're better educated, more financially independent, living longer, and in charge of our futures—but are we happier?" Not only have there been great advances for women, there have been great tragedies as a result of the changing mores of society. As might be expected, there has been a sharp rise in marital infidelity, in the number of unstable homes, and in the emotional, insecure environment for children. Often "things" have replaced the tender care of a mother, so important to the developing life of a child and adolescent. The article reported, "By 1999, just over half of all children under 12 years of age (1.6 million) were in some type of formal and/or informal child care. University of Tasmania research in 2001 showed that one in three Australian women, between the ages of 30–34 was without a partner" (*Ibid.*). The article comes back to the issue of happiness.

Many women battle with the problem of daily fatigue, as they try to combine a paid job with looking after their home and family. A large number admit to using anti-depressants or sleeping pills to relieve tension, and many say they feel guilty about the quality of their mothering (*Ibid.*).

Here are some of the startling but hardly surprising statistics showing the dramatic changes between 1933 and 2003: Children born out of wedlock in 1933, 5%; 2003, 31%. Keep in mind that the use of contraceptives in 1933 was rare, abortion was illegal and rare. In 1933 there were 1,954 divorces. In 2001 there were 55,330 divorces. Even factoring in that there are almost three times the number of inhabitants in Australia today as in 1933, this is an alarming increase of over seven times the number of divorces. Remember, ninety-five percent of parents were then legally married. Today that figure is sixty-nine percent.

We must not ignore other factors on the opposite side of the equation. In 1933, contraceptives, as we know them today, were unknown. The performing of permissive abortions resulted in jail terms of between five and seven years, and as for the doctors who performed those abortions, not only did they serve a significant prison term, their medical registration was cancelled, and that in turn was reported to quite a number of nations around the world.

We must also take into account today the number of women who live in common-law relationships, which is far beyond the situation in 1933. There is sufficient evidence extracted from this report, which in turn was taken from the Australian Bureau of Statistics and the Australian Census information, to deduce that modern life has resulted in large-scale unhappiness. Surely this is a major warning to all young people to seek an entirely different lifestyle and to follow "old fashioned" practices, which are far more in line with the principles of the Word of God.

The secularization of Australian society is highlighted by the fact that in 1933, 91% of weddings were conducted as religious ceremonies. In 2003 only 47% of weddings were conducted as religious ceremonies. Modern society has brought increased prosperity and a remarkable increase in standards of living, but it has greatly eroded the principles of the Christian family and has led to untold anguish and other negative consequences. We can only imagine how it has contributed to misery in homes, to depression and other forms of emotional illness, suicide, crime, antisocial behaviors, and the development of generations of parents who are increasingly incompetent in the education and training of their children.

The chief principles of the home are to be found in the inspired writings of the Scriptures. For a Christian, divorce is not an option. To grow up in a home where children have not the slightest fear that there may be a collapse of the marriage of their parents, is very strengthening to the security and emotional stability of the child. Urgently needed is a generation of young people from stable homes. Decisions must be made about the most appropriate role for the wife if children are to be initiated into the world. For untold generations, the mother has been the stable security of the home. Character, preparation for eternal life and training for Christian service are such impelling goals to Christian parents that they would rather live in great simplicity, and perhaps be seen as deprived of the wonderful inventions of man in this modern age, than to sacrifice their children to the idols of this world. Any sacrifice made now for the sake of the children will surely be abundantly rewarded in the eternal home.

27
Divorce in the United States

MATERIAL on the website of "divorcemagazine.com" reveals a litany of the carnage that results from divorce. One of the most dangerous features of today's society is the fatherless home. The report (2003) noted that fatherless homes in America account for 63% of youth suicides, 90% of homeless runaways, 85% of children with behavioral problems, 71% of high school dropouts, 85% of youth in prisons, and over 50% of teen mothers. Irresponsible fathers are one of the major causes of societal ills today. So often one is informed that the breakup of a marriage was best for the children. Statistics strikingly prove that such an assertion is false.

It is hard to envision a marriage so dysfunctional that it causes more serious injury to youths than the fatherless home. Those wives opting for separation and divorce, claiming it to be in the best interest of the children, ought to rethink the situation. Both spouses decide to accept the responsibility of parenthood. They then have a responsibility to do everything possible to hold a marriage together, and also to do all to provide a stable and complete environment for their children.

The issue of divorce and common-law partnerships continues to contribute to the breakdown of the Biblical family life. For example, between 1990 and 2000 there was a meager seven percent increase in married-couple families. Contrast this with the following during the same period. There was a seventy-one percent increase in unmarried-partner households, twenty-five percent increase in female-headed, single-parent families; sixty-two percent increase in male headed, single-parent families and twenty-one percent increase in single-person families (*The Visitor*, January, 2005, p. 7).

Divorce inevitably has its foundation in the selfishness of at least one of the partners. In this sensual and profligate age, many men, and increasing numbers of women, are trapped in the grip of evil. Passions will rise when men and women are separated from God, for the conscience is seared and their motives focus upon selfishness, lust and promiscuity. It is so difficult to bring up a family with two parents in the world of the Twenty-first Century, let alone with one parent.

So dysfunctional are some homes that neither parent takes responsibility for the guidance of the children. In many places it is the grandparents or other relatives who have to assume the responsibility to rear the children. Other children are in foster care and sometimes are passed around from one foster home to another. It is far more likely that children in these situations will develop into dysfunctional human beings and often repeat the behavior of one or the other of the parents. In some cases their lives are shattered by the irresponsibility of parents.

For too many, marriage is seen as a respectable way to legitimize sexual relations. The high and holy principle called love, built upon Divine instruction, is far from the thoughts of those who marry primarily for sexual gratification.

Here are some statistics which should be carefully considered by those seeking to forge a marriage. There were 1,163,000 divorces in the United States in 1997. In 1998 there were 19,400,000 divorced people in the United States. The median duration of the marriage of those divorced was 7.2 years (1998). The average age at which divorce occurs: 45.6 years for males and 33.2 for females (1998). Forty-three percent of weddings in 1997 involved at least one spouse who was beginning a second marriage. Almost 50% of first marriages end in divorce (1997), and 60% of remarriages end in divorce (1997). Age at marriage affects the marriage breakup rate. Of marriages where the spouse is under twenty, 40% break up early. When the marriage takes place at the age of 25, only 24% break up early. This indicates that immature marriage decisions significantly increase the likelihood of divorce. If the parents have divorced, there is a greater likelihood of divorce taking place in their children's marriages. Wives from broken homes divorce at the rate of 43% in the first ten years of marriage. Wives whose parents have remained married divorce at the rate of 29% in the first ten years.

Another interesting factor is that smokers are more likely to divorce, 49% compared with 32% of non-smokers. Perhaps those who take more care of their health are more responsible in the marriage relationship.

In 2001 the divorce rate was almost half that of the marriage rate. The marriage rate was 8.4 per 1,000 in the population. The divorce rate was 4.0 per 1,000.

On the website of Americans for Divorce Reform, it was reported that a survey of experienced divorce lawyers gave the following causes for divorce: 1) poor communications; 2) financial problems; 3) lack of commitment to the marriage; 4) infidelity. Other lists stated: 1) spouse failed to meet the expectations of the other spouse; 2) addictions and substance abuse;

3) physical, sexual, or emotional abuse; 4) lack of conflict resolution skills.

As in the Australian study where there has been a rapid increase in divorce rates over the last few decades, so in the American study. It was reported that between 1970 and 1996 the number of divorcees had increased from 4.3 million to 18.3 million, a quadrupling of the number of divorcees. There is no way to begin to evaluate statistically the impact of marital breakdown upon the decline in morality, the rise of crime, emotional instability, and other effects.

It was also reported that a variety of studies suggest the seeds of marital breakdown in divorce are already there when couples say "I Do" at the altar. This again reiterates the contention that divorce is greatly increased by inadequate preparation for marriage, and the lack of true principles in the courtship process. See the chapter entitled "I Do."

To the best of our knowledge, there are no statistics to show the economic impact, upon society and the nation, of divorce. In many cases, the wife (or husband) left with growing children may find that the only financial resource available is government support. While the other spouse almost always will be assessed financial responsibilities to the children and sometimes to the wife, large numbers fail to fulfill these obligations. While governments can be active in tracing down those who default on their financial commitments to the family, nevertheless, in reality only a small percentage are brought to accountability, and some of them continue to refuse, even preferring to accept other forms of legal penalties rather than to support the family.

As reported in divorcemagazine.com, 85% of divorced women have lower standards of living than before the divorce. This means that many of them have to seek government assistance because of their situations. Also, there is the cost of treatment for the emotional and sometimes physical consequences of divorce, which adds even further to the massive national bill.

When dealing with statistics, many factors are hard to ascertain. For example, while the cause of divorce may be stated by both spouses, often the most critical cause is overlooked for a cause which sounds more respectable or acceptable to the interviewer, who may be a counselor, a lawyer, family or friends. This makes it all the more difficult to evaluate all the factors contributing to the breakup of a marriage, separation, or divorce. However, we can say confidently that selfish motives and behavior are inevitably involved somewhere.

The magnitude of the social ills and the financial implications are horrific, when we consider that in the United States now over 2.5 million divorces take place annually. This affects 5 million adults besides the children involved. All told, there are approximately 10 million persons directly involved. Some are children and youth at a very vulnerable age. However, affected family and friends extend far more widely. Experts have estimated that the significant negative effect of every divorce, on average, impinges upon about 40 people. These include extended family such as parents, grandparents, uncles, aunts, nephews, nieces and close friends. If this figure is accurate, it means that up to 100 million people are affected by divorces every year. While that figure may appear to be too high, and certainly the level of emotional trauma will vary significantly, it does indicate the intensity of the carnage.

Sadly, under these circumstances many people take sides either for the wife or the husband. Friendships of long standing may be broken, leading to isolation from other friends. It is very difficult for many people to be able to have the same warmth of fellowship and relationship which they had in earlier times. The consequences of divorce are frightening.

We must add to this the not-well-established figures of those who are living together for periods of time, and the traumas of breakups among such ones. Lack of attention through childhood and adolescent years plays heavily into the carnage of divorce.

Our plea is for massive Bible-based education of parents in their responsibility for training their sons and daughters, so they will be better prepared for the sacred responsibility of matrimony. However, we acknowledge that the task of a major worldwide reform is overwhelmingly daunting because of the manifold factors and the widespread amorality in contemporary society. Therefore Christian parents have a most serious responsibility to minimize the evil effects of the permissive culture of the twenty-first century rather than reflecting these evils.

Tragic it is that in not a few nations, the statistics for divorce of church-going professing Christians is little distinguishable from those of their God-disdaining neighbors. The cruel reality is that worldliness has found a dominant haven in most Christian churches; priests, ministers, elders and deacons bear a large responsibility for this sorry state. Many of these men are involved in pedophilia, homosexuality and adultery themselves and thus present a thoroughly unscriptural gospel of permissiveness to their parishioners, on the grounds of promoting understanding, inclusiveness and love. The use of the word *love* in this manner is a perversion of the word. Only Satan rejoices when such family-destroying, misery-engendering love is promoted in church.

28

Divorce Is Ugly

LMOST all divorces result in enormous and wide-spreading consequences. As we have seen, it is estimated that an average of forty people suffer significant negative consequences from one divorce. This includes the spouses themselves, any children of the marriage, the parents of the spouses, the uncles, the aunts, the cousins, the nephews, the nieces, the grandparents, also the friends of the divorcees and often fellow church members. We repeat that a significant consequence is that often those involved with the divorcees take sides supporting one or the other. Many a friendship is broken with one of the spouses when divorce takes place. It is especially true when, not uncommonly, the divorce is bitterly contested by the spouses.

The most common and devastating effects of divorce are upon the children, the severity depending upon age: the damage may be less to a very young child. Even so, bringing up a child in a one-parent home, or with a step-parent, may have unanticipated consequences.Upon the child who has reached school age, the adverse effects of the divorce are considerably increased. Children are sensitive enough to feel guilty about the fact that their parents have divorced. For some reason, numbers of children of divorced parents develop a sense of guilt, believing that they have contributed to the divorce. They can also feel great alienation, for when a parent separates from their lives they experience great loss. This leads them to various degrees of insecurity, believing that the parent who has left does not love them. This has increasing consequences as the child grows into teenage years.

Colin, some years ago, met a seventeen-year-old young lady about to commence her senior year in boarding academy. When she was very young, her mother had left the family. Her truck-driver father gallantly sought to fill the vacuum. But as his driving often took him away for days, even his noble efforts were inadequate to fill the void in this child's life as she grew into her adolescent years. Because of the insecurity of the situation, father and daughter resided with the paternal grandmother. She too did her best to fill the void left by the departed mother, but the uncertainty remained.

On only a few occasions did she meet her mother after the early years. She was now seventeen. She had a great yearning in her heart for the mother to show love toward her. Earlier that year she had sent her mother a mother's day card. To her great joy her mother wrote her a short note in response. But no loving sentiments were expressed, no motherly interests were shared, nor did the mother, in that short note, give any evidence that she was interested in the progress of her daughter.

When Colin spoke with the young lady, her question was agonizing She had responded to her mother's letter but two months had passed since that response and there was no further contact from the mother. With tears and anguished voice she asked Colin, "Do you think my mother loves me?" It was one of the hardest answers that Colin had ever been required to give to a teenager. Of course, he did not say, "No, she doesn't love you." Rather he said, "How thankful you must be for a grandmother and a father who love you. Certainly God loves you," while letting her know that he could not know the answer to her question.

It is only natural for children to crave a mother. Mothers are God's gifts to children. They crave those softer, tender elements of what is a normal bonding between a mother and a child. It is rare that fathers can duplicate the same tender connection, especially with their daughters.

Here are some of the ugly issues which children face as a consequence of divorced parents.

1.   One spouse has to take the major responsibility, sometimes the total responsibility, for the raising of the children. There is no way that one spouse can be both father and mother to the children. The lack of a father in the home is devastating, especially to boys, and it is another consequential factor increasing the possibilities of developing homosexual tendencies in young men. Mothers are often unable to handle the needs of boys as they grow into the preteen and teen years, and such boys often take advantage of this in ways which are totally counterproductive to their adolescent years and indeed for the rest of their lives. Vice versa, a girl growing up without a mother lacks the modeling that is needed for a secure developing female and this can increase the likelihood of lesbian tendencies developing.

Anne Hooper, in her book *Divorce and Children*, made the following observation.

> Children of divorce often marry young themselves—perhaps in an attempt to recreate the family life that they felt was cut out from them as youngsters, perhaps as a method of escaping from what had been an uncomfortable home background.   Hooper, Anne,
> *Divorce and Children,* 1981, George, Allen and Unwin, London, p. 38.

Colin recalls meeting a nineteen-year-old academy senior at a college day. She told him that she planned marriage after graduation. Soon she explained that her parents had divorced years before, later her mother died and her father was in the process of divorcing for the third time. She was a very sincere young lady but it was obvious why she was rushing into an early marriage. She stated also that her fiancé was from a broken home. Colin explained her haste and counseled her to delay for at least two years. Colin also counseled likewise the young man, who he learned worked at the college where he served. They followed the counsel and today have a grown family and a stable Christian home.

Boys need a good father model to teach them what it is to be a man: strong, hard working, protective, yet loving and kind. Girls need the model of a good mother, tender, caring and deeply interested in the development of her child's character. It is no surprise to psychiatrists, clinical psychologists, social workers and counselors that so many children from one-parent homes have great identity crises, especially as they launch into the adolescent years. Almost all children of divorced parents suffer these consequences at least to some extent. Some profit from the blessing of strong modeling from a grandparent. Others develop well because of the bonding with a good step-parent who proves to be greatly solicitous of the children of the other spouse. However, all too frequently, such ideal situations do not take place. Not infrequently in a divorce situation both parents battle for the affection of the child. Often this is done by demeaning the other partner or trying to fill the child's mind with negative feelings for the other spouse. Children become the political football in such situations. It becomes especially difficult for the immature child who is desperately seeking to love each parent, when one or both parents are seeking unconditional love bonding with the child at the expense of the other parent. When the child is in the custody of the other parent and then returns home, and expresses happy reflections concerning the time he or she has spent with the other parent, jealousy, anger and negative comments are engendered from the legal custody parent. Unfair as it is to the child, nevertheless, that is not an uncommon situation, because often divorced parents have a high level of insecurity and immaturity and therefore they seek security through the unconditional, exclusive love of the child.

2.   In some marriage breakups the emotional shattering of one of the spouses leads to an overdependence upon the child for emotional and other forms of support. Colin recalls his dialogue with a young lady in California. This young lady was in her early twenties when Colin dialogued with her. Her mother, from her description, was almost dysfunctional. This young

lady told Colin that she, from early teenage years, had had to be a mother to her mother. That is too heavy a responsibility for teenagers to have to fulfill.

3.   Frequently, today, grandparents have to take over the care of the child from a broken home. This in itself can sometimes cause great custody battles. Both sets of grandparents are determined to have the parental responsibilities over the children. So often these situations occur when the grandparents are in middle life. They have brought up their own children, they have gone through the joys and sorrows of child rearing. They have reached an age where they are looking for a more comfortable situation with less stress and less burdens in their middle life as their physical and emotional energy often is in decline. Add to this that some middle-aged grandparents are now in higher levels of responsibility in the work place and they do not always make the very best parents. Even when they have been good parents to their own children, there is a tendency for grandparents to be more indulgent than young parents. This is partly due to their lowered energy levels, but it is also due to their concerns for the stress that the children are feeling as the result of the divorce of their parents.

If both mother and father are determined to have the custody of the children, the child has to go through a terrible war, and during the custody battles very frequently there is great uncertainty as to the legal result determining which spouse will be granted custody. Sometimes custody is given to a spouse with whom the child would prefer not to be. Later, as the child reaches into middle adolescence, judges are prone to reverse custody to the other spouse if the child prefers that. It is a most complicated situation because this results in unsettled adolescents, often not yet committed to settled values or religious convictions. Such youths will often choose the spouse less competent, the one who is easier to get on with, the spouse who will indulge the child and will reduce the necessary constraints for youth. This can lead to disastrous consequences.

4.   Frequently, somewhere along the life journey of the child of a divorce, he or she has to adjust to a new step-parent or, alternatively, a live-in partner. This has deep ramifications. If it be a live-in partner, the obvious immorality of such a situation and its effect upon the developing value system of the child can be greatly consequential to their own moral life, to their own instability, to their ability, in later life, to form a stable and enduring marriage. Often such ones themselves are being programmed to follow the erratic behavior of the parent even though they themselves have abhorred the circumstances in which they find themselves.

5.   The abuses of children by a new spouse or partner can be very severe. This can take the form of physical, verbal, sexual and/or emotional abuse. Some second spouses or partners develop a great jealousy over the affection of the mother or father for the children. This competition results from the selfish goals of the new step-parent. Thus children are treated with scant respect and often are treated brutally.

6.   Often there is a rapid decline in the scholastic achievement of children as the result of the divorce. A number of factors may contribute to this consequence. Of course, the emotional upheaval in the life of the child in itself distracts the child from academic concentration. Sometimes the teachers are unaware of the circumstances. Yet alert teachers should be in a position to realize that when there is a relatively sudden change in behavior or academic performance, one possible cause could be breakup in the family. If teachers are unaware of these circumstances they can add to the strain on the child by the teacher taking and demonstrating, albeit in ignorance, an unsympathetic attitude to the child who already is bowed down by grief over the home situation. The teacher may further add to the child's despair by taking unreasonable disciplinary measures. However, there are other factors in the school situation. Many children, when their parents are divorcing, feel greatly ashamed of the situation. They are afraid that their peers will learn about it and will somehow see them as inferior to the others who come from stable homes.

7.   Children from divorced homes are much more subject to abnormal behavior patterns, which can take the form of joining gangs, committing crimes, running away from home, seeking early sexual experiences and also early marriages or cohabitation.

8.   Juvenile incest is more likely to occur from a step-parent than with a genetic parent.

9.   The insecurity, the uncertainty, the emotional immaturity which so often occurs in the children of divorce leads to a much higher rate of juvenile suicide. So often young people think, "I am so unhappy and miserable, life is not worth living" that the only way out they see is to take their own lives.

10.   Children of divorced parents have a higher incidence of accidents and accidental deaths. This is often expressed in their tear-away use of vehicles. Their insecurity, frustrations, anger, lack of self-worth, all combine together to cause recklessness or to seek momentary excitement. It is much more difficult to teach responsibility to children of divorce, than to secure young people, and certainly sixteen years of age is an early age for such unstabilized young people to have the emotional and social maturity which is necessary for safe driving. They are much more likely to seek to take risks and attempt other dangerous endeavors. Often the so-called thrill seekers are insecure young people.

11. When the doubling of "parents" takes place it is often too much for young people. They have a father and a step-mother and a mother and a step-father and they find the complexity of such circumstances difficult to handle. If there are multiple divorces, the situation becomes even more complex. Colin had been talking to students at a boarding academy on the topic of "How to Have a Happy Marriage." He thought that he had provided some very important and easily understood principles for these young people. However, after one presentation, a seventeen-year-old young man sought him out. His question was as simple as it was short: "How do you have a happy marriage?" Colin did a little prying and learned that the young man's thirty-six year old mother had just married for the ninth time. So impossible did this seem to Colin that he approached the principal after the dialogue and explained to the principal what the young man had said. The principal's response was, "I don't know how many marriages there have been, but there has been just one succession of men in the life of his mother." Here, on the average of every two years of his life, he had to adjust to a new "father." Colin felt almost helpless. All he could do was to repeat the biblical principles of husbands and wives and fathers and mothers. What kind of a life has this young man had subsequently? How brutal it is for such insecurity to be thrust upon a child, for he was the child of the first marriage.

12. There are other consequences to divorce, outside the consequences to children of the divorcees. After all, many marriage breakups have not involved any children. However, in today's divorce settlements, most western countries mandate a fifty percent division of the assets of the family. There are few marriage breakups which do not have deep financial consequences for those involved. For example, for those who are purchasing a home, there is a great dilemma. The home now has to be sold unless an equitable agreement can be made. The selling of the home leaves neither with strong, viable assets, depending upon how close to completion is the payment. Especially women suffer in divorces, and routinely, the economic viability of divorced wives is seriously compromised. Most have great struggles and difficulties to support themselves, let alone their children.

13. If there are children in the equation, then the determination of alimony by a court insures that frequently great financial responsibility for the children is expected to be shared, and the spouse who is not awarded the child or children will frequently suffer the consequences of financial deprivation on the basis of the alimony assessments. Thus serious financial crises may result.

While this list is not all-inclusive, nevertheless it is a list which would make any responsible spouse reconsider any thoughts of separation and divorce. Divorce begins in the mind with dissatisfaction and is reinforced by actions and words. For a converted Christian, divorce would not be an option except for the most diabolical problems in the marriage relationship. A faithful Christian will seek to find God's way to maintain a loving, stable, enduring marriage.

29

Hope for the Fallen

WE have come to the end of this book. We believe that words of encouragement are in order. Some of you, perhaps most of you, have concluded that you would have done some things very differently in the past had you known and followed the instruction in this book. Colin well remembers a 19-year-old young lady who attended one of the colleges where he served as president. After a disastrous experience which had caused her indescribable pain, shame and remorse, she told Colin how she wished she had followed the earnest counsel of her parents. However, she passed through a rebellious period in which, by association with worldly youth, she had soon been led into the immorality of her peers. She was eaten up with great self-recriminations and she believed that her future was bleak. She believed that she was wholly unworthy of expecting to marry the kind of Christian man whom she now, after her conversion, desired. She believed she had so tarnished her moral character, and her reputation was so well known in church circles in which she moved, that no worthwhile young man would be the least interested in joining his life together with hers.

Knowing a little of the church community to which she now was joined in membership, Colin pointed out that, to the contrary, there was much joy and love for this young lady whose transformation of life had engendered great respect when, in her despair, she had turned back to the Lord. These people admired her courage and they quickly recognized her transformation of character. They saw her as a shining example of the power and grace of Christ, not only to recover, but to restore the young lady to the image of her Maker.

> He will turn again, he will have compassion upon us; he will subdue our iniquities: and thou wilt cast all their sins into the depths of the sea.   Micah 7:19

> And they shall teach no more every man his neighbor, and every man his brother, saying, Know the Lord: for they shall all know me, from the least of them unto the greatest of them, saith the Lord: for I will forgive their iniquity, and I will remember their sin no more.   Jeremiah 31:34

> As far as the east is form the west, so far hath he removed our transgressions form us. Psalm 103:12

It was evident that this young lady fully believed those texts. She also believed other passages of Scripture containing abiding promises for the fallen. These include:

> The Lord is not slack concerning His promise, as some men count slackness; but is longsuffering to us-ward, not willing that any should perish, but that all should come to repentance. 2 Peter 3:9

> Wherefore he is able also to save them to the uttermost that come unto God by him, seeing he ever liveth to make intercession for them. Hebrews 7:25

> All that the Father giveth me shall come to me; and him that cometh to me I will in no wise cast out. John 6:37

Colin discovered that she also had fully accepted these promises by faith, but what still troubled this young lady was her uncertainty that fellow human beings would accept her for what she now was, rather than what she had been when she was walking in the folly of her mid-teen-aged youth. It is true that there will be some who will likely feel compelled to spread to others the sins of our youth. Even there is the likelihood that some, believing that they are doing the right thing, will spread the story of one's past to a suitor, should courtship develop.

Colin's counsel to this young lady, and it would be our counsel to those reading this book who may have a sad past, to explain to the friend, soon after the friendship develops toward serious intentions, some details of the past life without getting into overly specific details. It is then up to the friend to decide whether the past outweighs the present character. This response will be a measure of the love that the suitor has for you. There is a great risk in remaining silent. You will find yourself living in a state of fear that someone else will reveal your past and cause a serious rift between the two of you after marriage. Further, it is only fair that the one who is contemplating becoming your spouse be able to evaluate all factors prior to making the life-long commitment for life-long marriage.

We realize that it can be an agonizing decision to express your past. It is not easy to know at what point in the relationship this would be best. Some have decided to wait until there is a proposal of marriage. At this point, the young lady may say, "There are some things which happened in my past which it is only fair that you should know before we make any commitment to each other." If "the past" is that of the young man it would be honorable for him to say something such as, "I desire to ask you if you will consent to marry me. However it is only fair to you that I reveal to you some of the mistakes I made in my earlier life before I ask that question."

It is our experience that godly young people, understanding the character transformation of the life of the one they have learned to love, will readily respond positively to the honesty of the other. Sometimes both the young man and the young woman will have revelations to make.

However, long before the proposal, much prayer and study of Bible principles must go into making the decision. The two must take into account all the important issues which have been discussed in this book. Premature proposals may lead to disastrous consequences.

We have written this book because we do not want sincere young people to make so monumental a decision as marriage with inadequate knowledge of what key issues must be considered, or to make the decision without thorough counsel from godly, experienced men and woman. We are facing the last moments of this earth's history. The Bible clearly foretells the fearful tests, trials and afflictions which God's people will confront in these latter days. It is also at this time that God has promised to fill His people with the power of the Holy Spirit.

> And it shall come to pass afterward, *that* I will pour out my Spirit upon all flesh; and your sons and your daughters shall prophesy, your old men shall dream dreams, your young men shall see visions: And also upon the servants and upon the handmaids in those days will I pour out my spirit. And I will shew wonders in the heavens an in the earth, blood, and fire, and pillars of smoke. The sun shall be turned into darkness, and the moon into blood, before the great and terrible day of the Lord come. And it shall come to pass, that whosoever shall call on the name of the Lord shall be delivered: for in mount Zion and in Jerusalem shall be deliverance, as the Lord hath said, and in the remnant whom the Lord shall call.   Joel 2:28–32

> Then shall we know, if we follow on to know the Lord: his going forth is prepared as the morning: and he shall come unto us as the rain, as the latter and former rain unto the earth.   Hosea 6:3

> Be patient therefore, brethren, unto the coming of the Lord. Behold, the husbandman waiteth for the precious fruit of the earth, and hath long patience for it, until he receive the early and latter rain.   James 5:7

It is the latter rain power of the Holy Spirit, which will empower all God's children, especially the young people, to proclaim the everlasting gospel to every human being in this planet as Jesus foretold.

> And this gospel of the kingdom shall be preached in all the world for a witness unto all nations: and then shall the end come.   Matthew 24:14

> And he said unto them, Go ye into all the world, and preach the gospel to every creature.   Mark 16:15

> And I saw another angel fly in the midst of heaven, having the everlasting gospel to preach unto them that dwell on the earth, and to every nation, and kin-

dred, and tongue, and people, Saying with a loud voice, Fear God, and give glory to him; for the hour of his judgment is come; and worship him that made heaven, and earth, and the sea, and the fountain of waters.   Revelation 14:6–7

God is calling each of you to be part, not only of His kingdom, but of His faithful witnesses. In the marvelous power of the Holy Spirit, you will take His final invitation to men and women, encouraging them to surrender their lives to Christ so that they may live eternally with Him.

It is our earnest prayer that you all will be there and we will have that joy of living with you for eternity. We further pray that in this short time before the glorious return of Jesus, you will be guided by the Lord in the choice of a life-companion who will share with you the joy of service for God, and who will encourage you, while you encourage him or her, to walk in the footsteps of Jesus. May your home be a witness to the power of Christ and a witness to others in your community. May it be a foretaste of heaven.

Scriptural Index

Genesis
    2:1–3 10
    2:21–24 10
    19:4–5 66
    49:4 63
Exodus
    20:4–5 80
    20:14 6
Leviticus
    13:20 119
    18:22 66, 119, 125
    18:23 67
    20:13 124
Deuteronomy
    10:12, 13 37
Judges
    14:1–3 41
1 Kings
    16:31, 32 41
Psalms
    103:12 145
    119:11 51
    139:13–16 40
Proverbs
    6:24–29 64
    6:34 77
    13:15 65
    14:12–14 65
    18:22 33
    19:14 33
    21:17 67
    22:6 32
    23:31–34 67
    31:10–31 34
The Song of Solomon
    8:6 77
Isaiah
    3:16–24 56
    49:1 39
    55:2 78
Jeremiah
    1:5 40
    9:2–3 64

Jeremiah (continued)
    17:9 110
    31:34 144
Hosea
    6:3 146
Joel
    2:28–32 146
Micah
    7:6 74
    7:19 144
Matthew
    5:8 79
    5:28 6, 50, 52, 89
    5:48 23
    6:33 48
    11:11 39
    18:3 76
    19:9 65
    19:14 76
    19:24 20
    19:26 24
    24:14 146
Mark
    16:15 146
Luke
    1:15 39, 81
    1:41 39, 81
    1:67 30, 81
    16:8 55
    17:28–30 66
John
    5:30 24
    6:37 145
    14:20 25
    15:5–7 25
    17:17 23
Acts
    2:1 23
Romans
    1:16 127
    1:24, 26 66
    1:26–27 119, 125
    1:27 67, 119

Romans (continued)
    1:31–32 119, 124
    12:2 117
1 Corinthians
    6:9 67, 75, 119, 125
    7:12–14 73
    10:13 123
    10:31 75
    14:20 76
2 Corinthians
    3:18 79
    6:14 58, 83
Ephesians
    4:12–15 23, 76
Philippians
    2:3 46
    2:5 24, 50
    4:8 79
1 Timothy
    1:10 119, 125
    2:9, 10 56
    6:9 8, 49
    6:10 77
2 Timothy
    2:21 49
    2:22 8, 49
Titus
    2:12 49
Hebrews
    7:25 145
James
    1:8 63
    4:7 25, 123, 126
    5:7 146
1 Peter
    1:22 24
    2:11 50
    3:3, 4 56
    4:1, 2 53
    5:8 45
2 Peter
    1:4 24, 50
    2:6 66

Syllabus

An adjunct to the General Index, featuring paragraph titles.

Chapter 5: What Are the Marriage Stakes?
1. Much is at stake
2. Eternal destinies are at stake
3. Great tragedies have resulted from broken homes
4. Emotional health of individuals is at stake
5. Divorce influences generations unborn.
6. Affluence
7. Jesus' return delayed.

Chapter 8: Counsel to Parents
Maintain fair but firm parameters.
Guard carefully regarding peer group pressure.
Do not permit early dating.
Be prepared to resist pressure from the children.
Firm but not emotional guidance.
Guard against "puppy love."
Train children to be a blessing to others.
Train children to reach out.

Chapter 11: Qualities to Look For In a Husband
See pages 44–48.

Chapter 15: Bible Principles Which, If Ignored, Contribute to Divorce
1. Responsibility
2. Morality
3. Sexual Rectitude
4. Sobriety

Chapter 17: Other Bible Principles Which, If Ignored, Contribute to Divorce
5. In-laws
6. Ill health
7. Immaturity

8.   Jealousy
9.   Finance
10. The Hollywood Myth

Chapter 18: Other Risk Factors

1.   Marrying young
2.   Lack of Common Interests
3.   Financial Responsibility
4.   Different Religious Value Systems
5.   Poor Communications
6.   Self Centeredness
7.   Influence of the Media
8.   Preparation for Marriage
9.   Addictions

Other behaviors which take place before marriage which also contribute to the heightened risk of divorce:

a.   Familiarity and frivolity with the opposite sex
b.   Dating around with a number of those of the opposite sex.
c.   Premarital Sex
d.   Pornography
e.   Homosexuality and Lesbianism
f.   Children of Divorced Parents
g.   Working Wives
h.   Physical Abuse
i.   Sexual Abuse
j.   Verbal Abuse

Chapter 19: Consequences for Children of the Divorced

1.   Unpredictable environment for the children
2.   Separation of one parent from the children
3.   "Bribing" of children to gain their affection away from the other divorcee
4.   Hidden emotions of children of divorce.
5.   Insecurity, fears, broken hopes.
6.   Revelations of faults of the parents
7.   Remarriage of one parent dashes children's hope of restored home.
8.   Remarriage often brings other children into the home.
9.   Remarriages subject to breakup.
10. Separation of siblings
11. Children often denied contact with one parent
12. Children of deserted wife often in poverty.

13. Parent with custody may become obsessive toward children
14. Divorced parent may become involved in common-law partnership
15. Children of divorce often develop behavioral and social problems
   a. Bedwetting, nightmares, withdrawal, aggressive behavior, excessive sleep.
   b. Confusion, tell different versions
   c. Difficult to make friends
   d. Likely to early sex
   e. Mother's discipline sometimes weak
   f. Children feel shame for the divorce
   g. Decrease in scholastic performance
   h. Child may become moody, sullen, aggressive, suicidal, homicidal, may join gangs.
   i. Immature and dangerous independence
   j. Feel betrayed, unloved by divorcing parents
   k. Distance themselves from home
   l. Parents may have less time, less attention for children
   m. Young marriages

General Index

(SEE SYLLABUS for chapter outlines)

selflessness : 30
senior administrative roles : 101
sexually transmitted disease : 107,
　　113, 114
shame, feelings of great : 99
signs, subtle : 14
sin, gain victory over : 125
single-minded focus : 98
Smalley, Dr. Gary : 107
social mores : 5, 6, 109
sports : 85
St. Mary's Hospital in London : 6
step-parent substitute for the
　　divorced parent : 96
teacher's attitude : 141
Ten Commandments : 5
Ten Percent (homosexual) : 120
thrill seekers : 142
to the altar pure : 110, 113
Toney, James : 107
touching : 88
trifle (with love) : 88

U
ugly issues facing children : 138
unequally yoked together : 29, 57–62
unfeigned love : 24
unity of the faith : 23
unrealistic view of marriage : 79
unsafe driving : 142
unwanted pregnancy : 107, 112

V
venereal disease : 7, 114
Victoria, Queen, discredits lesbianism
　　: 123
victory, power of : 25
virginity, virtue of : 113
visit regularly a nursing home : 32
visitation rights limited : 94

W
wife deserted : 97
wife forced into workplace : 90, 97
women's revolution : 128
Wycliffe, John : 20

Y
young marriages : 99

Z
zinc deficiency : 51

Books by Colin and Russell Standish
(Unless otherwise noted as by one or the other)

The Antichrist Is Here   **$10.95 PB 185 pgs.**
A newly updated, second edition! Colin and Russell Standish have extensively researched the historical identification of the Antichrist of past generations and are convinced the Antichrist is present on earth now. A must read for those who are interested in Biblical prophecy and its outworking in contemporary history.

The Big Bang Exploded   **$11.95 PB 218 pgs.**
A refutation of the Big Bang theory and Darwin's proposal of natural selection, which boldly presents evidence that the authors assert supports, far more closely, the fiat creation concept than the evolutionary model.

Education for Excellence   **$11.95 PB 176 pgs.**
This book goes directly to the word of God for educational principles for the sons and daughters of the King of the Universe.

The Entertainment Syndrome   **$11.95 PB 125 pgs.**
This book explores how the large increase in entertainment impacts the physical, emotional, social, intellectual and spiritual life of the human race, and the devastating effect of its use in our churches.

The Evangelical Dilemma   **$10.95 PB 222 pgs.**
There has never been a more urgent time for an honest review of the past, present and future of evangelical Protestantism. The authors present an examination of the major doctrinal errors of Evangelical Protestants.

Georgia Sits On Grandpa's Knee (R. Standish)   **$7.95 PB 86 pgs.**
Stories for children based on the experience of Russell and his children in the mission field.

God's Solution for Depression, Guilt and Mental Illness
                                           $12.95 PB 229 pgs.
This powerful book argues with great persuasiveness that God is interested in every aspect of His created beings and that the perfect answers to man's needs are to be found in the Word of God.

Grandpa, You're Back! (R. Standish) $9.95 PB 128 pgs.
Pastor Russell Standish again delights and fascinates his granddaughter,
Georgia, with stories of his many travels to countries ranging from South
America to such far-flung places as Singapore, Africa, and beyond. These
stories should pleasantly awake the imagination of young readers.

Gwanpa and Nanny's Home (R. Standish and Ella Rankin)
                                              $14.95 PB 128 pgs.
"I am Ella Marie Rankin. I want to tell you about Gwanpa's and Nanny's
home. But I have a problem! You see, I'm only three and I haven't yet
learned to write. So, my Gwanpa is writing my story for me." So begins
a book that Russell Standish wrote for his granddaughter.

Liberty in the Balance $14.95 PB 285 pgs.
The bloodstained pathway to religious and civil liberty faces its greatest test in 200 years. The United States Bill of Rights lifted the concept
of liberty far beyond the realm of toleration to an inalienable right for
all citizens. Yet, for a century and a half, some students of the prophecies of John the Revelator have foretold a time just prior to the return
of Christ when these most cherished freedoms will be wrenched from
the citizens of the United States, and the U.S. would enforce its coer-
cive edicts upon the rest of the world. This book traces the courageous
battle for freedom, a battle stained with the sufferings of many mar-
tyrs.

The Lord's Day $15.95 PB 317 pgs.
The issue of the apostolic origin of Sunday worship had often been a
contentious one between Roman Catholics and Protestants. This book
presents an in-depth examination of the Sabbath in Scriptures.

Modern Bible Translations Unmasked $13.95 PB 244 pgs.
This book will challenge the reader to consider two very serious problems with modern Bible translations: first, the use of corrupted Greek
manuscripts; and second, translational bias. This is a must read for anyone interested the veracity and accuracy of the Word of God.

The Mystery of Death $10.95 PB 144 pgs.
There are those today who believe that the soul is immortal and eter-
nally preexisted the body. Pagan or Christian, the opinions vary widely.
In this book, the history of these concepts is reviewed and the words of
Scripture are investigated for a definitive and unchallengeable answer.

Perils of Ecumenism $15.95 PB 416 pgs.
The march of ecumenism seems unstoppable. From its humble roots after
the first World War, with the formation of the Faith and Order Council
at Edinburgh University, Scotland, and the Works and Labor Council at

Oxford University, England, to the formation of the World Council of Churches in 1948 in Amsterdam, it has gained breathtaking momentum. The authors see the ecumenical movement, very clearly identified in Holy Scriptures, as the movement devised by the arch-deceiver to beguile the inhabitants of the world.

The Pope's Letter and Sunday Law   **$7.95 PB 116 pgs.**
This book presents a detailed examination of John Paul II's apostolic letter, "Dies Domini."

The Rapture and the Antichrist   **$14.95 PB 288 pgs.**
This book sets forth the plainest truths of Scripture directing Protestantism back to its Biblical roots. It will challenge the thinking of all Christians, erase the fictions of the *Left Behind* Series, and plant the reader's spiritual feet firmly on the platform of Scripture.

*The Rapture, the End Times and the Millennium***$15.95 PB 378 pgs.**
This book will open the minds of the readers to a clear understanding of areas of the end time which have led to much perplexity among laypersons and theologians alike. It is also guaranteed to dispel many of the perplexities presently confronting those who are searching for a clear Biblical exposition of the last cataclysmic days in which we now live.

The Second Coming   **$7.95 PB 80 pgs.**
The Apostle Paul refers to the Second Coming of Jesus as the blessed hope (Titus 2:12). Yet, soon after the death of all the apostles, doubts and debates robbed the people of this assurance and brought in the pagan notion of immediate life after death. In this newly updated work, Colin and Russell Standish present a wake-up call for every complacent Christian.

Two Beasts, Three Deadly Wounds and Fourteen Popes
          $16.95 PB 331 pgs.
The Book of Revelation has been characterized as a mystery. Yet, the book describes itself as the "Revelation of Jesus Christ" (Revelation 1:1). In this book, the authors, using Scripture as its own interpreter, unravel aspects of the mystery and unveil a portion of the revelation.

Youth, Are You Preparing for Your Divorce?   **$11.95 PB 168 pgs.**
A majority of youth, including Christian youth, are destined for divorce. Yes, you read this correctly! Unbeknown to them or to their parents, long before marriage or even courtship, the seeds of divorce have been sown to later produce their baneful consequences. Many youth who think they are preparing for marital bliss are preparing for divorce and, all

too frequently, their parents are co-conspirators in this tragedy. The authors provide amazingly simple principles to avert the likelihood of future divorce.

Youth Do You Dare! (C. Standish) $9.95 PB 88 pgs.
If you are a young person looking for workable answers to the many issues that confront you today, this book is for you. It presents a call to young people to follow truth and righteousness, and to live morally upright lives.

Other Books from Hartland Publications

Behold the Lamb - David Kang $8.95 PB 107 pgs.
God's plan of redemption for this world and the preservation of the universe is revealed in the sanctuary which God constructed through Moses. This book explains the sanctuary service in the light of the Christian's personal experience. Why this book? Because Jesus is coming soon!

Christ and Antichrist - Samuel J. Cassels $24.95 HB 348 pgs.
First published in 1846 by a well-known Presbyterian minister, who called this book "not sectarian, but a Christian and Protestant work." He hoped that the removal of obstacles might result in a more rapid spread of the Gospel. One of these obstacles he saw as "Antichristianity," a term that he used to describe the Papal system.

Distinctive Vegetarian Cuisine - Sue M. Weir $14.95 PB 329 pgs.
100% vegan cooking, with no animal products—no meat, milk, eggs, cheese, or even honey. No irritating spices or condiments are used. Most of the ingredients can be found at your local market. There are additional nutritional information and helpful hints. Make your dinner table appealing to the appetite!

Food for Thought - Susan Jen $10.95 PB 160 pgs.
Where does the energy which food creates come from? What kinds of foods are the most conducive to robust health and wellbeing in all dimensions of our life? What is a balanced diet? Written by a healthcare professional, this book examines the food we prepare for our table.

Group Think - Horace E. Walsh $5.95 PB 96 pgs.
Find out how a state of groupthink (or group dynamics) has often contributed to disaster in secular and spiritual matters, like the role of Hebrew groupthink in the rejection and ultimate crucifixion of the Son of God, or the ecumenical movement that seeks to unite the minds of

dedicated men so strongly that their passion is to build one great super church following Rome.

Heroes of the Reformation - Hagstotz and Hagstotz
$14.95 PB 307 pgs.

This volume brings together a comprehensive picture of the leaders of the Reformation who arose all over Europe. The authors of this volume have made a sincere endeavor to bring the men of Protestantism alive in the hearts of this generation.

History of the Gunpowder Plot - Philip Sidney $13.95 PB 303 pgs.

Originally published on the 300th anniversary of the November 5, 1605 plot aimed at the destruction of the English Realm, this book is Philip Sydney's account of one of the most audacious conspiracies ever known to the ancient or modern worlds. The failed plot became part of English popular culture.

The History of Protestantism - J. A. Wylie
$99.95 PB 4 Volumes, PB 2,136 pgs.

This book pulls back the divine curtain and reveals God's hand in the affairs of His church during the Protestant Reformation. Your heart will be stirred by the lives of Protestant heroes, and your mind captivated by God's simple means to counteract the intrigues of its enemies. As God's church faces the last days, this compelling book will appeal, and will be a blessing, to adults as well as children

History of the Reformation in the Time of Calvin - d'Aubigné
$129.95 4 Volumes, PB 1,971 pgs.

The renovation of the individual, of the Church, and of the human race, is the theme. This renovation is, at the same time, an enfranchisement; and we might assign, as a motto to the Reformation accomplished by Calvin, as well as to apostolical Christianity itself, these words of Jesus Christ: "The truth shall make you free" (John 8:32).

History of the Waldenses - J. A. Wylie $12.95 PB 191 pgs.

During the long centuries of papal supremacy, the Waldenses defied the crushing power of Rome and rejected her false doctrines and traditions. This stalwart people cherished and preserved the pure Word of God. It is fitting that this edition of their history should be reprinted to keep alive the spirit and knowledge of this ancient people.

Hus the Heretic by *Poggius the Papist* $9.95 PB 78 pgs.

One of the greatest of Reformers in history was John Hus. His pious life and witness during his trial and martyrdom convinced many of the priests and church leaders of his innocence and the justice of his cause. Poggius was the papal legate who delivered the summons to Hus to appear at the council of Constance, then participated as a member. This book consists of letters from Poggius to his friend Nikolai, and describes the trial and burning of Hus. So potent was John Hus' humble testimony, that some even of his ardent foes became his defenders.

The Law and the Sabbath - Allen Walker $9.95 PB 149 pgs.
A fierce controversy is swirling around the role the Ten Commandments should play in the church of the 21st Century. With a foreword by the late Elder Joe Crews, here is a book that dares to examine the Bible's own answers—with unfailing scriptural logic and a profound appreciation for the doctrine of righteousness by faith.

The Method of Grace - John Flavel $14.95 PB 458 pgs.
In this faithful reprint, John Flavel thoroughly outlines the work of God's Spirit in applying the redemptive work of Christ to the believer. Readers will find their faith challenged and enriched. In true Puritan tradition, a clearly defined theology is delivered with evangelistic fervor by an author urgently concerned about the eternal destiny of the human soul.

The Reformation in Spain - Thomas M'Crie $13.95 PB 272 pgs.
The boldness with which Luther attacked the abuses and the authority of the Church of Rome in the 16th Century attracted attention throughout Christendom. Luther's writings, along with the earlier ones of Erasmus, gained a foothold with a Spanish people hungry for the truth. Thomas M'Crie makes a case for a Spain free of the religious errors and corruptions that ultimately dried up the resources and poisoned the fountains of a great empire.

Romanism and the Reformation - H. Grattan Guinness
                                                  $12.95 PB 217 pgs.
The Reformation of the 16th Century, which gave birth to Protestantism, was based on Scripture. It gave back to the world the Bible. Such Reformation work needs to be done again today. The duty of diffusing information on the true character and history of "Romanism and the Reformation" is one that presses on God's faithful people in these days.

Strange Fire - Barry Harker $11.95 PB 206 pgs.
The Olympic games are almost universally accepted as a great international festival of peace, sportsmanship, and friendly competition. Yet, the games are riddled with conflict, cheating, and objectionable com-

petitiveness. Discover the disturbing truth about the modern Olympics and the role of Christianity in the rise of this neo-pagan religion.

Truth Triumphant - **Benjamin George Wilkinson $16.95 PB 440 pgs.**
The prominence given to the "Church in the Wilderness" in the Scriptures establishes without argument its existence and emphasizes its importance. The same challenges exist today for the Remnant Church in its final controversy against the powers of evil to show the holy, unchanging message of the Bible.

Who Are These Three Angels? - **Jeff Wehr $6.95 PB 126 pgs.**
The messages of three holy angels unfold for us events that are soon to take place. Their warning is not to be taken lightly. They tell of political and religious movements that signal the soon return of Jesus.

Youth Ministry in Crisis - **Barry Harker $10.95 PB 156 pgs.**
In this bracing book, Dr. Harker examines the practices and passions that are transforming and debasing contemporary youth ministry—rock music, magic, clowning, comedy, drama, mime, puppetry, sports, extreme adventure activities, youth fashions and movies—and exposes the disturbing ideas that permit them to flourish in God's church. Dr. Harker also outlines steps that need to be taken if the enveloping crisis is to be resolved and youth ministry restored to a culture of defensible innovation. This book is a timely corrective to the ideas and practices that are defacing the image of God in His people.

True Education History Series
from Hartland Publications

Livingstone—The Pathfinder - **Basil Matthews $8.95 PB 112 pgs.**
Like most boys and girls, David Livingstone wondered what he would become when he grew up. He had heard of a brave man who was a missionary doctor in China. He also learned that this Dr. Gutzlaff had a Hero, Jesus, who had come to people as a healer and missionary. David learned all about this great physician, and felt that the finest thing in the whole world for him was to follow in the same way and be a medical missionary. That was David's quest and his plan. Between these pages, you will see how he made his good wish come true.

Missionary Annals—Memoir of Robert Moffat - **M. L. Wilder**
$7.95 PB 64 pgs.
Robert Moffat first heard from his wise and pious mother's lips that there were heathen in the world, and that the efforts of Christians sharing

the knowledge of a Savior could raise them out of their base degradation. An intense desire took possession of him to serve God in some marked manner but how that would be, he did not know. Through a series of providential circumstances and in God's good time, the London Society accepted him as one of their missionaries, and in 1816, he embarked on his first trip and got his first glimpse of heathen Africa. This book will inspire young and old as you read the many trials, disappointments, triumphs, and wondrous miracles that God can accomplish when one is fully surrendered to Him.

The Waldenses—The Church in the Wilderness   **$8.95 PB 68 pgs.**
The faithful Waldenses in their mountain retreats were married in a spiritual sense to God who promised, "I will betroth thee unto me in faithfulness and thou shalt know the Lord" (Hosea 2:20). No invention of Satan could destroy their union with God. Follow the history of these people as they are compared to the dedicated eagle parents.

Meet the Authors

Colin D. Standish (L) and Russell R. Standish

COLIN and RUSSELL STANDISH were born in Newcastle, Australia, in 1933. They both obtained their teaching diplomas from Avondale College in 1951. They were appointed to one-teacher elementary schools in rural areas of New South Wales, each teaching for three years.

In 1958, both completed a major in history and undertook an honors degree in psychology at Sydney University in the field of learning theory. Colin continued obtaining his Master of Arts degree with honors in 1961, and his Doctor of Philosophy in 1964. His Masters Degree in Education was completed in 1967.

Russell graduated as a physician in 1964. Six years later he was admitted to the Royal College of Physicians (UK) by examination. He was elevated to the Fellowship of the Royal Colleges of Physicians in Edinburgh (1983) and Glasgow (1984).

In 1965, Colin was appointed Chairman of the Education Department at Avondale College. Subsequently he held the posts of Academic Dean at West Indies College (1970–1973), Chairman of the Department of Psychology, Columbia Union College (1974), President of Columbia Union College (1974–1978), and Dean of Weimar College (1978–1983). He was invited to become the foundational president of Hartland Institute, which comprises a degree-issuing college, a wellness center, publishing house and a world mission division.

Russell as a Consultant Physician (Internist) has held the posts of Deputy Medical Superintendent of the Austin Hospital, University of Melbourne (1975–1978), President of a hospital in Bangkok (1979–1984), Medical Director at Enton Medical Centre, England (1984–1986), and President of a Penang hospital (1986–1992). Since 1992 he has been speaker and editor for Remnant Herald. As well, he is presently Administrator of Highwood College and Health Centre in Narbethong, Victoria, Australia.

They have co-authored more than forty-five books.

HARTLAND Publications was established in 1984 as a conservative, self supporting Protestant publishing house. We publish Bible-based books and produce media for Christians of all ages, to help them in the development of their personal characters, always giving glory to God in preparation for the soon return of our Lord and Savior, Christ Jesus. We are especially dedicated to reprinting significant books on Protestant history that might otherwise go out of circulation. Hartland Publications supports and promotes other Christian publishers and media producers who are consistent with biblical principles of truth and righteousness. We are seeking to arouse the spirit of true Protestantism, one that is based on the Bible and the Bible only, thus awakening the world to a sense of the value and privilege of the religious liberty that we currently enjoy.

Office hours: 9:00 a.m. to 5:00 p.m. Mon. – Thurs.
9:00 a.m. to 12:00 noon Fri. (Eastern time)

You may order by telephone, fax, mail, e-mail or on the web site

Payment in US dollars by check, money order, most credit cards
Order line: 1-800-774-3566; FAX 1-540-672-3568

Web site: www.hartlandpublications.com
E-mail: sales@hartlandpublications.org